MG CLASSICS

Book 3

1965-2001

by Eric Dymock

Based on The MG File, an Eric Dymock Motor Book by Dove Publishing,
Old West Kirk Manse, 31 Argyle Terrace, Rothesay, Bute PA20 0BD in 2001. © Eric Dymock 2001.
ISBN 978-0-9574585-9-8 (was 0 9534142 3 X)

This completely revised updated edition produced in Great Britain by Dove Publishing Ltd.
5 Abbey Park, Torksey, Lincoln LN1 2LS

ISBN Amazon paperback 978-0-9574585-9-8

Visit www.dovepublishing.co.uk to read more about our books and author.

CONTENTS

MG's model range widened to include refined sports coupes like the MGB GT.

MG HISTORY: from 1965

By the 1960s it looked, for a time, as though the British Motor Corporation understood MG better. The MGB was successful and joint production of Austin-Healeys and MG Midgets well established. The Competitions Department set up at Abingdon was making a name for itself in racing and rallying for the entire Corporation especially Mini. Yet the bigger picture of the UK motor industry as a whole was at best uneven. It had developed untidily, in haphazard groupings ill-suited to repel an onslaught approaching from imports of high-quality reliable and stylish cars in particular from the Far East and principally Japan.

In 1968 Leyland Motor Corporation and British Motor Holdings (BMH) joined up to create the second largest car manufacturer outside the United States. The organization that became known as the British Leyland Motor Corporation (BLMC or BL) was composed of the old British Motor Corporation's Austin, Morris, Riley, Wolseley and MG, together with Leyland's Standard-Triumph, Rover, Scammell, AEC and Thornycroft. Following BMC's takeover of Pressed Steel, which was making its bodies, Jaguar joined as well, bringing with it Daimler and Guy and a wide inventory of cars, trucks and buses. BL's combined sales were over £800m, it had a market value of £412m, 52 per cent of UK home sales and about 60 per cent of British vehicle exports. These were worth £250m and, for a while, rising. On the face of it there seemed no stopping its path to prosperity even though the BMC car makes were already looking the weaker end of the business. The heavy end, led by Leyland was strong in trucks and buses especially following the additions of Daimler, AEC and Guy.

Yet crucially when Ford, traditionally with some of the best cost-analysts in the industry, examined what looked like one of BL's great assets, the Mini, it revealed that its maker was losing £30 on every one it made. Notwithstanding such doubts, a deal was stitched together under Harold Wilson's Labour administration's Industrial Reorganisation Corporation (IRC) established in 1966 to promote the efficiency and competitiveness of British industry. "Picking winners in the white heat of new technology," was how the jargon of the time put it. Led by board members that included Labour activist Geoffrey Robinson who became MP for Coventry North West in 1976 and subsequently Paymaster General in 1997-1998 the IRC lent British Leyland Motor Corporation £25m. Robinson had been a success at Innocenti the Italian factory making Sprites and was later put in charge of Jaguar.

Left: Sir Donald Gresham Stokes
(1914-2008 later Lord Stokes)

BL chief executive was Donald Stokes, former chairman of Leyland, who had made a name for himself selling buses to the world. He was eager to pay tribute to the Minister of Technology who had inspired the arrangement, one Anthony Wedgwood Benn (1925-2014), as he was known after relinquishing his title of Viscount Stansgate. Sir George Harriman (1908-1973), former BMH executive chairman was appointed chairman of the British Leyland Motor Corporation.

The amalgamation of Austin and Morris into BMC in 1952 had been difficult enough. Loyal Morris executives and Austin executives had been rivals and never agreeable. But that was nothing compared to the jumble of BLMC's manufacturing units up and down the country. Often competing with each other, few were well managed and almost all worked under the fractious industrial relations that dogged much of the industry well into the 1970s. Following a change of government in 1970 the IRC was largely dismantled, Ford and Vauxhall prospered at the expense of the British Leyland marques and when Labour returned to power in 1974 Sir Don Ryder (later Lord Ryder of Eaton Hastings 1916-2003, formerly a financial journalist) was appointed to report on a loss-making industrial muddle long propped up by the taxpayer.

It was a difficult brief. Ryder was to form a rescue plan for BL, which had begun to face financial embarrassment from further weakening of its position in the market. Secretary of State for Industry, now Tony Benn, called on Ryder to report by March 1975 and while this concluded, "We do not subscribe to the view that all the ills of BL can be laid at the door of a strike-prone and work-shy labour force," it had to acknowledge that labour disputes one way or another lay at the root of the problem. Industrial action trebled between 1971 and 1974. BL's 170,000 employees worked in 60 plants in eight divisions, belonged to 17 different unions and had 246 separate bargaining units. The Advisory Conciliation and Arbitration Service (ACAS) set up in 1975 was faced with reconciling not only unions and management, but also unions and unions. It was now widely assumed BL would in due course be nationalised but the British Leyland Shop Stewards' Committee, recognised by neither side and led by Derek Robinson (1927-2017), the infamous "Red Robbo", was dissatisfied. The Trade Unions wanted management by joint committees, nominated half by them and half by the government, but since the government nominees were themselves under pressure from the unions Ryder rejected this. Instead he put in place management councils with two levels of joint committees.

This was not much better.

A lot of the Ryder report was never implemented and in 1975 the government took a majority of British Leyland shares through the National Enterprise Board (NEB), effectively at last nationalising it. Lord Ryder remained chairman of the NEB but even he was unable to prevent the disastrous unofficial toolroom strike in the winter of 1977, when 40,000 workers were laid off. This cost BL £150m, and 700 disputes lost the output of 250,000 vehicles, a quarter of that year's production. The NEB became identified with failing state-owned companies and its financial guarantees encouraged increasingly ambitious union demands bearing no relationship to productivity, quality or profitability. It was a planning system derided by government minister Michael Heseltine as, "A vehicle for marauding socialism."

Tony Benn talked of providing £3bn and making 750,000 cars a year, but Lord Ryder became enmeshed in the infamous BL "slush fund" scandal and left the NEB in July 1977. The entire episode was a token of how futile political meddling in industry could be. Dirigiste governments mostly although not exclusively Labour, all invoked disasters that destroyed much of the indigenous car industry. A generation would pass before incoming investors, often from abroad, would restore it.

Following Harold Wilson's resignation in 1976, James Callaghan became prime minister and in October 1977 South African Michael Edwardes (b 1930 and later Sir Michael) a member of the National Enterprise Board was put in charge of BL. Edwardes claimed, "The Ryder remedy only produced a bureaucratic paperchase dissipating management resource and effort." Edwardes boldly tackled union militancy, sacked a lot of management and shut down 13 factories, including Speke on Merseyside, Triumph at Canley, Rover Cars at Solihull and, most controversially, MG at Abingdon-on-Thames. His plans were rejected by the Transport and General Workers' Union (TGWU) so BL conducted a postal ballot in which 80 per cent of workers voted. Of these 87 per cent were in Edwardes' favour.

In November 1979 Edwardes' campaign led to Austin-Morris's vigorous CEO Harold Musgrove bravely firing Red Robbo and securing 20,000 votes backing him and reversing a trend that had threatened the entire industry. Edwardes left in 1982 with BL smaller, slimmer, allied to Honda but transformed and viable. Strikes were reduced to manageable numbers, new working practices introduced, working days lost declined and the number of vehicles missing through industrial action came down to 28,000. A hundred thousand MGAs and half a million MGBs had come out of the little factory at Abingdon. Celebrations surrounding the fiftieth year of production at the plant in Berkshire (or in Oxfordshire after 1974) turned within days to dismay, when Edwardes announced its closure. The nationalised corporation claimed it was losing £900 on every MGB it made, but there was widespread disbelief. It seemed more likely that the figure was an accountant's fiction and MG simply had never fitted in with Stokes' and Triumph-dominated BL's plans. It was scant reward for the 1100-strong workforce's exemplary industrial relations, but Edwardes could see no future for the symbiotic relationship Cecil Kimber had forged half a century earlier between sports cars and volume cars.

A consortium led by Alan Curtis, chairman of Aston Martin, tried to mount a rescue. Curtis recruited an unlikely member, Lord George Brown Labour foreign secretary 1966-1968, describing him darkly as "invaluable behind the scenes". Others included Peter Cadbury, chairman of Westward TV, and David Wickens of British Car Auctions, but its bid was rejected. In any case BL refused to relinquish the MG title which, like Rover, still had a ring to it. The last MGB came off the line at Abingdon on 23rd October 1980, after which the factory was closed, sold off and the site redeveloped.

In 1988 the government disposed of BL to British Aerospace for £150m. Its subsequent sale in 1994 to BMW for £800m was testimony either to the progress that had been made, or else the price had been too low. In the end even BMW was unable to cope and BL was offered back to a handful of its managers for a nominal £10.

MG in the meantime had gone into a sort of suspended animation. For a while it had been no more than a soubriquet applied to sporting versions of BL cars, not all of them unworthily, until the mid-1980s when MG re-emerged under a more inspired Rover-led stewardship. Its return from oblivion was careful and well-managed. A turning point came with the 1985 MG EX-E (below), a concept designed to show that MG was on its way back, not as a resuscitated backward-looking relic, but as a modern make of car fit for the 1990s.

In 1988 British Motor Heritage was created to make new bodies for MG classics, and introduced the RV8 in October 1992, 30 years after the introduction of the MGB. The rebirth of MG in the 1990s had drawn warm approval. It was a measure of the affection held for MG that, by the summer of 1992 when pictures were released of the RV8, speculation over PR3, codename for the MGF, was rife.

The RV8 took up where the MGB left off. It might have been more logical to start with an engine based on the stillborn O-series (there was a perfectly appropriate one, the M16 that used O-series bottom end and a splendid twin-cam head) but it was a time of cheap fuel and a revival of interest in classics like the AC Cobra. Rover, it seems, was apprehensive about down-sizing and drew inspiration from re-born classics with ever-larger engines.

Appearance of the MG RV8 at 1990s motor shows suggested that the classic era of MG was not yet entirely over.

Work was started on the MGF in partnership with Mayflower Vehicle Systems, a consortium that since 1991 included Motor Panels, the Coventry body-building company dating back to 1920 that had associations with MG through Tickford and the Coventry Hood and Sidescreen Company. Ten years elapsed between the EX-E and the MGF, during the period when BL had become Austin-Rover and been absorbed by British Aerospace. As Rover Group it forged a promising partnership with Honda, then in 1994 when it was sold to BMW there was heavy investment until it became apparent the group was never going to achieve the 500,000 cars a year necessary for a return to profit.

Under Bernd Peter Pischetsrieder, its highly-regarded CEO, BMW saw an opportunity for a luxury brand to complement its Munich range of essentially speed-oriented products. It introduced the splendid Rover 75 but many of the old successor managers lately of British Leyland were still in place. Austin people and Morris-Wolseley-Riley-MG people had never got on in BMC days and now Standard-Triumph people and Rover people were added to the mix and still fell out with one another. Bureaucracy and complacency ruled and, in the end, BMW could not wait to rid itself of what the German press called, "the English patient".

During negotiations between BMW and likely buyers a conference was called at Downing Street under Geoffrey Norris, the Cabinet Office's industrial expert. City analysts and industry leaders dismissed a plan put up by John Towers and the incumbent directors known, not very imaginatively, as Phoenix. In car manufacturing, apparently, you either had to make 500,000 a year to compete in the volume market, or 50,000 a year in a high-unit-profit niche segment. Straddling both at 200,000 a year was not a profitable option, as Jaguar might have testified.

Jon Moulton and his partner in a rival bid from Alchemy Partners (inspiring names were thin on the ground at the end of the 1990s) proposed it should relinquish the Rover name, and redevelop MG to manufacture small numbers at premium prices. This would have turned it into a specialist sports car maker, making perhaps the essential 50,000 and, while there would have been redundancies, Professor Sir Kumar Bhattacharyya of Warwick University, adviser to the then Transport Secretary Stephen Byers supported the Alchemy plan. Professor Bhattacharyya said later: "I don't believe 99.9 per cent of the opposing takeover coalition (workforce, trade unions, and politicians who were supporting Towers and Phoenix) understood what they were doing. They were doing it purely for emotional and social reasons. Moulton had a plan that was articulated. I was on the Rover task force and could not see what other plan would work."

Suspicion should have been aroused by the obsessive support of those abetting Towers, in particular the trade unions. If BMW could not make anything of Rover after spending £2.5bn on it, there was not much hope for hitherto undistinguished middle management. BMW made Towers and Phoenix the same offer it had to Moulton and Alchemy. It was so glad to see the back of Rover that it provided £500m working capital to take it away. Phoenix made an undertaking that only 2000 of the 8800 jobs at Longbridge would be lost, which explained the unions' enthusiasm, yet BMW never believed Towers would be able to make a go of it. The German firm did not want the opprobrium of leaving Rover to fail but knew perfectly well that in due course, under Towers, it would fail anyway.

There was talk of 250,000 cars a year, a prediction scaled back to 200,000; more or less what Rover had been managing under BMW, but it was soon being pushed to manage 136,000 and in 2001 lost £95m. Astonishingly, the directors were still doing nicely. Soon after the buy-out from BMW, Towers and his group hived off MG Rover's profitable finance arm MGR Capital, owned jointly with Halifax Bank of Scotland (HBOS). Its annual turnover was £33m, and directors' rewards included £10m each of good loan stock. It was no wonder that even the trade unions became disillusioned, demanding an enquiry into an alleged £73m black hole in the workers' pension fund.

Towers moved, by motor industry standards, with the speed of light. An entirely new range of cars was planned as the company tried to balance the books. The new programme saw MG variants of Rovers introduced by Towers and his deputy chairman Nick Stephenson, former Rover chief engineer and then a senior director of Huntingdon racing car manufacturer Lola. They had been clear about policy before the ink was dry on the May 2000 agreement with BMW. In July they recruited talented Peter Stevens, another former colleague at British Leyland, to oversee the design of new MGs. Stevens, whose creative credentials included the Jaguar XJR 15, Lotus Élan, and the £650,000 McLaren F1, was soon at work on a series of MGs based on existing Rovers as well as a flagship supercar for the 24 Hours Le Mans race.

Recalling the badge engineering from which British Leyland suffered, Towers was reassuring: "Forget the MG Maestro and MG Montego. These new cars will have different driving dynamics from Rovers and a degree of real performance. The whole experience of owning an MG will be special." He had not overlooked the historical precedent for MGs emerging as developments of an existing saloon and touring range. Cecil Kimber's principles for MG were merely being reapplied, and all Rover's 300 British dealers were automatically offered the MG franchise.

Introducing Rover models at the 1997 Paris Motor Show, Towers strikes a reassuring pose

Towers paid tribute to the quality and integrity of what cars the new group inherited. The engineering flexibility of the platforms enabled designers to create new ones of strong sporting character, and BMW's quality measurement system was exemplary. MG-Rover's fortunes depended on husbanding its cash-flow, reorganising itself by concentrating activities on one site, Longbridge. Overheads under the old regime, which had had to bear the costs of engineers and executives commuting between Munich and Gaydon, the British technical centre, were removed.

Managing director, then chief executive of Rover up to May 1996, Towers could be expected to know what he was getting into. He had joined from Perkins as engineering director in 1988 and during his four-year tenure as MD Rover went from a loss of £49m to an operating profit of £92m. It seemed like the culmination of a transformation started more than a decade earlier by South

African Sir Michael Edwardes, Rover CEO 1977-1982 and Canadian Sir Judson Graham Day OC ONS CD QC, brought in after running nationalised British Shipbuilders to be CEO 1986-1991.

Significantly by then MG accounted for a quarter of MG Rover's joint output. Far from being a sideline product in a bigger organisation it had evolved into a major player. Its re-launch was a characteristic motor industry media extravaganza with loud music, dry ice, flashing lights, racy film and gleaming cars. It took place in dour Longbridge, inside the Exhibition Hall across Lowhill Lane from where trade union leader Red Robbo had held his paralysing mass meetings in the 1970s. Keynote speakers used hyperbole from which even politicians might have shrunk, claiming the new MGs would earn warm praise.

According to Rob Oldaker, product development director, work on new MGs had to be done clandestinely before the sale lest BMW could have regarded them as competitors. Now, it was claimed, they were to be more legitimately regarded as bargain BMWs appealing to keen drivers at prices starting under £10,000. It was fanciful.

By MG's eighth decade it had almost looked as though it might at last achieve some sort of independence. It said something for the deep foundations on which it was built that it had survived at all, a testimony to the integrity of the Kimbers and the Morrises, not to mention the Len Lords, Thornleys and Enevers. It was surprising that it had survived with any reputation worth speaking about yet for the time being MG and Rover were two of the best-liked names in British motoring. Their evil day had, alas, only been postponed. The directors' provision of a £13m pension fund for themselves was acknowledgement that the game was up. Like Saigon before the fall of South Vietnam it looked as though it was every man for himself and the rescue operation three years before, when Rover had been bought for the symbolic £10 in May 2000 was pure opportunism.

The 1970s evolution of British Leyland, government intervention, Lord Stokes's delusions of grandeur, nationalisation, privatisation, ownership by British Aerospace and the loss of Mini, Jaguar and Land Rover were over. So was the promising alliance with Honda that had been quickly repudiated by BMW. Honda and BMW had far too much in common at the quality and driving enthusiast end of the market ever to have been bed-fellows and MG really fitted in with neither. Buyers saw merit in the cars, right up to the point in spring 2000 when BMW gave up.

The Germans had just brought out one of the best Rovers ever, the splendidly smooth, quiet, and elegant 75, which ought to have sold in competition with the X-type Jaguar, or even the S-type. Instead, as credibility decayed, it languished in the bargain basement. Many were heavily discounted. The 75 should have sold on prestige; instead it was sold on price. Rover made little money on it, and its cosmetically enhanced MG versions (see overpage, Rover's last gasp at Geneva 2002) were no more convincing. The Indian-made Tata City Rover might have been just about feasible, but was lacklustre and over-priced. MG Rover's efforts to re-badge cars as MGs never worked, and while talented designer Peter Stevens made a passable effort at silk purses with only sows' ears to work on, failure loomed.

The company was no longer viable without a major partner, cheerfully admitting that without a Chinese deal it had no future. It was so short of cash that its research and development budget virtually ceased. There was no prospect of new models. Sales from the rump of a British Motor Corporation that once had 30 per cent of the British market had sunk to around 3 per cent. The Phoenix Consortium's loss for the last eight months of 2004 was estimated at £400m. This was reduced to around £80m by 2004 but it never made a profit. In 2001 it posted sales of 170,000, but by 2004 this had shrunk to 120,000.

MG had become a chimera. Some of Peter Stevens' designs based on old Rovers found buyers, yet their failure to sell in any numbers spoke volumes. Customers were no longer convinced. The Geneva Motor Show of 2005 got by for the first time without any MG or any Rover. The 75th Swiss show was the first ever at which no representative of the company that inherited the great names of the British motor industry, Austin, Morris, Wolseley, Riley, MG, Rover, Standard, Triumph, Alvis, Leyland or any of the others was present. MG Rover was apparently too busy trying to talk billions out of the Shanghai Automotive Industry Corporation (SAIC) to attend. Furthermore it claimed, "We have no new models to show," an inconvenience that had never prevented it before and in any case was untrue. There were suggestions that the sudden cancellation of its appearance was due to doubts over the company's ability to pay its entry dues to the Palais des Expositions.

The end of the road for MG Rover came on 7/8 April 2005. Patricia Hewitt, Secretary of State for Trade and Industry announced receivership and it ceased trading with debts of over £1.4bn. In its frenzy to avoid collapse ahead of a general election the New Labour government proffered a VAT holiday, exemption from National Insurance payments, and a £6.5m loan. It was never going to be enough and was certain to invoke the wrath of European competition laws.

The breakdown inevitably came with the loss of 6,000 jobs and in 2011 businessmen Peter Beale, Nick Stephenson, John Towers and John Edwards, the so-called "Phoenix Four" were struck off as company directors for a combined 19 years. They had shared £42m in pay and pensions after buying the company in 2000.

Accountants Deloitte had advised MG Rover on administration, but controversially also acted as corporate advisers to the buyout group. In a 2013 judgment, the Financial Reporting Council's (FRC) tribunal said Deloitte had failed to manage the conflicts of interest created and, "showed in some instances a persistent and deliberate disregard of the fundamental principles and statements of the ICAEW's (Institute of Chartered Accountants England and Wales) ethics. Deloitte disagreed. "Deloitte's advice, which itself was not criticised, helped to generate over £650m of value for the MG Rover Group, keeping the company alive for five years longer than might have been the case and securing 5,000 jobs in the West Midlands. We take our client and public interest responsibilities extremely seriously and are proud of the value we helped create for the MG Rover Group," it said.

Left: Hardknot and Wrynose, Lake District passes beloved of British sports car drivers for generations, were traditional excursions for a long line of sports 2-seaters.

All that remained was for the Shanghai Automotive Industry Corporation (SAIC) to uproot the production line of the Rover 75 from Longbridge and set it up in China. It had been moved once already, from Cowley where it was set up under the BMW regime, so it was fairly portable. BMW refused to relinquish rights to the Rover and Mini brand names, which had only been licensed to MG Rover and had been sold to Ford, which bought Land Rover in 2000. The Chinese salvaged the MG title, the production facilities and some intellectual property but little more.

The classic era of MG was over.

MG CLASSICS MODEL by MODEL
from 1966

1966-1969 Midget Mk III GAN 4

The A-series engine dated from 1943, when Austin was instructed to look for an alternative power unit for Jeeps. Two cylinders were lopped off a 6-cylinder truck engine adapted for Austin's first post-war saloon, the Sixteen. Compacted down to 1.0 litre it went into 27 different BMC models placed both longitudinally and transversely, including the Austin A35 and Morris Minor, as well as Minis of various sorts to a total of some 13m made up to the 1990s. Overcrowding on the pushrod side meant siamesing the inlet and exhaust ports, common tracts leading to two valves, an arrangement of which combustion chamber consultant Harry Weslake profoundly disapproved. The engine was developed to 1071cc for the Mini–Cooper then, in 1964 with staggered cylinders for the 1275 Mini–Cooper S. This represented an increase from its original 803cc by some 60 per cent and developed 72bhp (53.7kW) but detuning enabled it to be made of cheaper materials. Placed lengthwise for the Midget it had smaller valves and a compression ratio of 8.8, against the Mini's 9.7:1 by virtue of dished piston crowns. Only the Cooper had the Nitrided E40 steel crankshaft, changed later following quality concerns to Tuftrided. The Midget III of October 1966 had a more sophisticated hood and a bigger cockpit aperture, yet the interior still seemed cramped as seats grew bigger and the bulkhead hampered their rearwards adjustment. Praiseworthy brakes and gearbox kept Midgets abreast of the market, but only just.

BODY sports, 2 doors, 2 seats; weight 1575lb (714kg). ENGINE 4 cylinders, in-line; front; 70.61mm x 81.28mm, 1275cc; compr 8.8:1 8.0 optional; 65bhp (48.5kW) @ 6000rpm; 51bhp (38kW)/l; 72lbft (97Nm) @ 3000rpm. ENGINE STRUCTURE pushrod ohv, chain-driven cam; cast iron cylinder head, block; 2 SU HS2 1¼ in carbs, SU electric fuel pump; 3-bearing crankshaft. TRANSMISSION rear wheel drive; 6½ in diaphragm spring sdp clutch; 4-speed manual gearbox, synchro; hypoid final drive 4.22 later 3.9:1. CHASSIS DETAILS steel platform chassis; ifs by coil springs and wishbones; live rear axle semi-elliptic 5-leaf springs, Armstrong lever arm hydraulic dampers; optional anti-roll bar; Lockheed hydraulic brakes 8¼in (20.9cm) disc front, 7in (17.8cm) drums rear; rack and pinion steering; 6gal (27.3l) fuel tank; 5.20–13 Dunlop tubeless tyres; steel disc wheels, wire wheels optional. DIMENSIONS wheelbase 80in (203.2cm); track 45.25in (114.9cm) front, 44.75in (113.7cm) rear; turning circle 30.1ft (9.2m); ground clearance 5in (12.7cm); length 135.25in (346.1cm); width 53in (134.5cm); height 49.75in (126.4cm). PERFORMANCE maximum speed 94mph (151kph); 15.4mph (24.7kph) later 16.5mph (26.5kph) @ 1000rpm; 0-60mph (96kph) 14.1sec; 11kg/bhp (14.7kg/kW); 29.6mpg (9.5l/100km) fuel consumption. PRICE £683 18s 2d (£683 90p). PRODUCTION 13,722.

D–reg 1966 launch publicity picture. Square-ish rear wheel arches rounded after 1972
and changed back again after they failed stern impact tests.

1965–1967 MGB GT

The Aston Martin DB2/4 of 1953 created a new kind of sports coupe better suited to autobahn speeds than open cars. By the 1960s fabric hoods had been made really wind-tight, but with no sound insulation to speak of they were noisy. Here instead was a pioneering secure steel-roofed hatchback with an opening rear window giving access to generous luggage space. A closed-top MGB was planned ahead of the B's announcement but Abingdon was so busy satisfying demand for the open car there was scarcely time or the resources to do it. MG was still being starved of investment. Besides, there was no consensus on the shape of those detachable hardtops that were popular.

Coachbuilders and hardtop-makers including Coune of Belgium tried to meet John Thornley's demand for a down-market Aston Martin. He might well have added E-type Jaguar, even though plans for an engine providing anything like Jaguar pace never came to fruition. When Syd Enever took a quarter-scale model of the proposal to Morris Bodies at Coventry to discuss manufacture, he was told that BMC had a long-standing arrangement with Pininfarina for things like that. Pininfarina's first effort at drawing one up was no better than Abingdon's and it was only when it was sent a full-sized MGB to work on that the result was successful. The key difference was the height of the windscreen. There was some argument about whether getting this right was an inspiration of Abingdon or Turin; either way the result was one of the best-proportioned cars of the day.

BODY coupe, 2 doors, 2+2 seats; weight 2379lb (1079kg). ENGINE 4 cylinders, in-line; front; 80.26mm x 88.9mm, 1798cc; compr 8.8:1; 95bhp (70.8kW) @ 5400rpm; 52.8bhp (39.4kW)/l; 110lbft (148Nm) @ 3000rpm. ENGINE STRUCTURE pushrod ohv; chain-driven camshaft; cast iron cylinder head and block; 2 SU inclined H4 carburettors, SU electrical fuel pump; centrifugal and vacuum ignition control; 5-bearing crankshaft; engine rubber-mounted; oil cooler. TRANSMISSION rear wheel drive; Borg & Beck 8in (20.3cm) diaphragm spring clutch; 4-speed manual gearbox, synchromesh; o/d optional 0.8:1; single-piece open prop shaft; Salisbury hypoid bevel final drive 3.91:1. CHASSIS steel monocoque structure; ifs by coil springs and unequal wishbones, anti-roll bar; live axle with semi-elliptic springs; Armstrong lever arm dampers; Lockheed hydraulic brakes, front 10.75in (27.3cm) discs, rear 10in (25.4cm) drums; rack and helical pinion steering; 12gal (54.6l) fuel tank; Dunlop C41 5.60-14 or SP41 165-14 tyres; 4½J rim wire wheels opt, 4J steel wheel rims.
DIMENSIONS wheelbase 91.75in (233cm); track 50in (127cm); turning circle 30.5ft (9.3m); ground clearance 5.25in (13.3cm); length 153.75in (390.5cm); width 60in (152.4cm); height 49.5in (125.7cm). PERFORMANCE maximum speed 107mph (171.8kph); 22.4mph (36kph) o/d top, 11.2mph (18kph) top @ 1000rpm; 0-60mph (96kph) 13.2sec; 11.4kg/bhp (15.2kg/kW); 20.9mpg (13.5l/100km). PRICE£998 8s 9d (£998 43.75p). PRODUCTION 125,621 all MGB GTs.

Five main bearing engine in Gaydon British Motor Museum MGB.

1967–1969 MGB

The MGB, like many cars with long lifespans, was subject to continuous change, especially during the Leyland years of cosmetic makeovers. One of the most significant amendments took place as a result of BMC engine policy. The old B-series was insufficiently smooth-running for the new Austin 1800, so from the 1965 model year it was provided with five main bearings instead of three. The change was accomplished without affecting the engine externally, so the mountings were unaltered but the extra bearings made it less free-revving. It was more refined and reliable but not so fast.

A 12 gallon (54.6 litre) fuel tank came in at the same time together with an all-synchromesh gearbox entailing a structural change to the transmission tunnel. An alternator replaced the dynamo in 1968 as more emission control measures came into play and American-specification cars brought increasing changes. Energy-absorbing dashboards and rocker switches were necessary to comply with new regulations and MG production suffered as resources were diverted to deal with them. The GT, with its stiffer springing and anti-roll bar, prospered, bringing the attraction of luggage accommodation 38in (96.5cm) wide by 30in (76.2cm) deep with the seat backrest up.

BODY roadster, 2 doors, 2 seats; weight 2030lb (920.8kg). ENGINE 4 cylinders, in-line; front; 80.26mm x 88.9mm, 1798cc; compr 8.8:1; 95bhp (70.8kW) @ 5400rpm; 52.8bhp (39.4kW)/l); 110lbft (147.5Nm) @ 3000rpm. ENGINE STRUCTURE pushrod overhead valve; chain-driven camshaft; cast iron cylinder head and block; 2 SU inclined H4 carburettors, SU electrical fuel pump; centrifugal and vacuum ignition control; 5-bearing crankshaft; engine rubber-mounted; oil cooler. TRANSMISSION rear wheel drive; Borg & Beck 8in (20.3cm) diaphragm spring clutch; 4-speed manual gearbox, all-synchromesh; automatic optional; single-piece open prop shaft; Salisbury hypoid bevel final drive 3.91:1. CHASSIS DETAILS steel monocoque structure; ifs by coil springs and unequal wishbones; live axle with semi-elliptic springs, optional anti-roll bar; Armstrong lever arm dampers; Lockheed hydraulic brakes, front 10.75in (27.3cm) discs, rear 10in (25.4cm) drums; rack and helical pinion steering; 12gal (54.6l) fuel tank; Dunlop Road Speed 5.90-14 tyres; 4J rims; wire wheels optional. DIMENSIONS wheelbase 91in (231.1cm); track 49in (22.9cm) (124.5cm); turning circle 30.5ft (9.3m); ground clearance 4.25in (10.8cm); length 153.75in (390.5cm); width 60in (152.4cm); height 49.25in (125cm). PERFORMANCE maximum speed 108.1mph (173.5kph); 16.4mph (26.3kph); 0-60mph (96kph) 12.1sec; 9.8kg/bhp (13kg/kW); fuel consumption 23mpg (12.3l/100km). PRICE £870 2s 3d (870 11.25p). PRODUCTION 513,276 all MGB.

Raised transmission tunnel was among modifications made necessary for the approaching introduction of the MGC. The space required for the all-synchromesh gearbox allowed the option of an automatic gearbox that continued until 1973.

1967–1969 MGC

The politics of BMC/British Leyland, which had brought in the Healeys, father and sons during LP Lord's time, banished them in Donald Stokes's. Yet Austin-Healey production remained important to Abingdon's commercial viability and a replacement was sought for the 3000, which Stokes wanted phased out at the end of 1967. A number of prototype schemes were launched, including some that continued to use the Healey name, but time was short and there was a good deal of pressure from American dealers to secure the succession. The result was a hurried compromise that, had it only been given time to mature, would have resulted in a perfectly satisfactory car. The basis, the substantial and strongly engineered MGB monohull in both open and GT form was already there and sufficient wit remained to produce a suitable 6-cylinder engine.

Once it had been decided not to use the existing BMC C-series, the Healeys fostered a move upmarket with a big 4.0litre Princess R Rolls-Royce engine. Morris Engines, faced with adapting a 6-cylinder for a forthcoming saloon as well as a sports car, drew one up but it turned out unsatisfactory for both. It was not much different from the abandoned C-series, its weight estimates were badly awry and a new floor pan would have been needed. Either way it had to have torsion bar front suspension because the cross member that picked up the coil springs would not fit under a 6-cylinder's sump. Too many compromises were necessary for success and with BL's customary ineptitude development work was hurried and inadequate.

BODY roadster, 2 doors, 2 seats; weight 2460lb (1116kg). ENGINE 6 cylinders, in-line; front; 83.36mm x 88.9mm, 2912cc; compr 9.0:1; 145bhp (108.1kW) @ 5250rpm; 49.8bhp (37.1kW)/l; 170lbft (228Nm) @ 3400rpm. ENGINE STRUCTURE pushrod ohv; chain-driven camshaft; cast iron cylinder head and block; 2 SU HS6 1¾in carburettors, SU electrical fuel pump; centrifugal and vacuum ignition control; 7-bearing crankshaft; engine rubber-mounted; oil cooler. TRANSMISSION rear wheel drive; Borg & Beck 9in (22.9cm) diaphragm spring clutch; 4-speed manual gearbox, all-synchromesh; single-piece open prop shaft; hypoid bevel final drive 3.307:1, optional Laycock LH overdrive 0.82:1, Salisbury final drive 3.7:1; optional automatic Borg Warner Type 35. CHASSIS DETAILS steel monocoque structure; ifs by unequal length parallel wishbones and torsion bars, with anti-roll bar; live axle on semi-elliptic springs; Armstrong telescopic dampers front, lever arm rear; Girling brakes, front 11.25in (28.6cm) discs, rear 9in (22.9cm) drums; Cam gears rack and pinion steering; 12gal (54.6l) fuel tank; Dunlop SP 41 165–15 tyres; 5J rims; wire wheels optional. DIMENSIONS wheelbase 91in (231.1cm); track 50in (127cm) front, 49.5in (125.7cm) rear; turning circle 36ft (11m); ground clearance 4.5in (11.4cm); length 153.2in (389.1cm); width 60in (152.4cm); height 49.25in (125.1cm). PERFORMANCE maximum speed 118mph (189kph); 27mph (43.3kph) o/d top; 22.1mph (35.5kph) direct top @ 1000rpm; 0-60mph (96kph) 10.0sec; 7.7kg/bhp (10.3kg/kW); 19.3mpg (14.6l/100km). PRICE £1101 16s 6d (£1101 82.5p). PRODUCTION 4542.

Above: author's picture of press launch at Gaydon, when the test track was

still for the most part a former Royal Air Force runway.

1967–1969 MGC GT

Bonnet bulge and fatter tyres apart, there was little to distinguish the MGC GT from the B, yet it felt quite different. With 55.7 per cent of its weight on the front wheels against the B's 52.5 per cent, the B's nimble handling was gone, and the MGC's splendid long-legged cruising qualities, like those of big Austin-Healeys withdrawn just when the C was announced, were only apparent on wide expanses of autobahn. Within two years the C was gone as well. University Motors, a long-standing MG dealer, in no doubt that it had not been at all bad, bought the last 141, comprising 118 GTs and 23 roadsters.

The MGC may have been best suited for wide open spaces, but it looked the part and rode serenely. University Motors remembered how demand had persisted for the MGA Twin Cam after it was stopped so instead of selling off the remaining MGCs cheaply, it sold them at a premium. With a Downton Stage II engine conversion it was priced at £1620 instead of £1386 and thus modified was a revelation. It retained the old Healey's strident appeal, the engine was smooth and powerful and although short on low-speed torque, acceleration was 20 per cent faster, and top speed 130mph

(208.7kph). There were cosmetic additions; a different grille and a small leather steering wheel instead of the standard over-large one. This exaggerated the heaviness of the steering at parking speeds but it looked good. If the MGC had been made as well as this in the first place there would have been no need to abandon it and the creators of the original B in the 1950s, who always wanted it to have more power, were thoroughly vindicated.

BODY coupe, 2 doors, 2+2 seats; weight 2615lb (1186kg) (automatic). ENGINE 6 cylinders, in-line; front; 83.36mm x 88.9mm, 2912cc; compr 9.0:1; 145bhp (108kW) @ 5250rpm; 49.8bhp (37.1kW)/; 170lbft (228Nm) @ 3400rpm. ENGINE STRUCTURE pushrod ohv; chain-driven camshaft; cast iron cyl head and block; 2 SU HS6 1¾in carbs, SU electrical fuel pump; centrifugal and vacuum ign control; 7-bearing crank; engine rubber-mounted; oil cooler. TRANSMISSION rear wheel drive; Borg & Beck 9in (22.9cm) diaphragm spring clutch; 4-speed manual gearbox, all-synchromesh; single-piece open prop shaft; hypoid bevel final drive 3.307:1, optional Laycock LH overdrive 0.82:1, Salisbury final drive 3.7:1; optional auto Borg Warner Type 35 final drive 3.35:1. CHASSIS steel monocoque; ifs by unequal length parallel wishbones and torsion bars, with anti-roll bar; live axle on semi-elliptic springs; Armstrong telescopic dampers front, lever arm rear; Girling brakes, front 11.25in (28.6cm) discs, rear 9in (22.9cm) drums; cam gears rack and pinion steering; 12gal (54.6l); Dunlop SP 41 165-15 tyres; 5J rims; wire wheels optional; 72-spoke optional. DIMENSIONS wheelbase 91in (231cm); track 50in (127cm) front, 49.5in (125.7cm) rear; turning circle 36ft (11m); ground clearance 4.5in (11.4cm); length 153.2in (389cm); width 60in (152.4cm); height 50in (127cm). PERFORMANCE max 120mph (193kph); 27mph (43.3kph) o/d top, 22.1mph (35.5kph) direct top and auto @ 1000rpm; 0-60mph (96kph) 10sec; 8.2kg/bhp (11kg/kW); 19.3mpg (14.6l/100km). PRICE £1249. PRODUCTION 4457.

Above: commendable University Motors MGC tested by Eric Dymock in 1969.

1968 MGC GTS Sebring racer

The last cars from BMC Competitions Department at Abingdon were ready before the 1967 production MGC on which they were based. Raced as prototypes, which meant they had to bear more than a superficial resemblance to the production version, the first, with a 2004cc MGB engine and 150bhp (111.9kW) @ 6000rpm, came ninth in the 1967 Targa Florio. In 1968 at Sebring 'Mabel' (MBL 546E) No44, driven by Paddy Hopkirk and Andrew Hedges, won its class, was third prototype and 10th overall with a 3.0litre engine. It also raced in the 84-hour Marathon de la Route on the Nürburgring and came sixth after a heroic performance by Tony Fall who drove two whole laps of the demanding 14.17mile (22.8km) Nordschleife without brakes.

Another car was built with an aluminium engine and they raced again at Sebring in 1969. It was the final appearance of works cars under the flag of British Leyland and not simply BMC. Number 35 (RMO 699F), driven by Hopkirk and Hedges, finished ninth prototype and 15th overall. Number 36 ('Mabel' 546E) driven by Craig Hill and Bill Brack, finished 15th prototype and 34th overall behind a private MGB driven by John Colgate and Don Parks. Although overshadowed, as category winners rather than outright overall champions, they endorsed the raceworthiness of the stiff adaptable B's hull just as effectively as the team prize in the Mille Miglia of 1933 had distinguished the K3.

BODY coupe, 2 doors, 2 seats; weight 2240lb (1016kg). ENGINE 6 cylinders, in-line; front; 84.1mm x 88.9mm, 2956cc; compr 9.0:1; 210bhp (156.6kW) @ 6000rpm; 71bhp (53kW)/l. ENGINE STRUCTURE pushrod overhead valve; chain-driven camshaft; aluminium cylinder head and cast iron block (one engine made with aluminium block); 3 twin choke Weber carburettors; centrifugal and vacuum ignition control; 7-bearing crankshaft; engine rubber-mounted; oil cooler. TRANSMISSION rear wheel drive; Borg & Beck 9in (22.9cm) diaphragm spring clutch; 4-speed manual all-synchromesh; single-piece open prop shaft; hypoid bevel final drive 3.307:1, Laycock LH overdrive 0.82:1, Salisbury final drive 3.7:1. CHASSIS steel monocoque structure; ifs by unequal length parallel wishbones and torsion bars adjustable from within; anti-roll bar; live rear axle on semi-elliptic springs with locating arms and anti-roll bar; Armstrong adjustable telescopic dampers; Girling disc brakes; Cam gears rack and pinion steering; 24gal (109.1l) tank; racing tyres, centre-lock alloy wheels. DIMENSIONS wheelbase 91in (231.1cm); track 50in (127cm) front, 49.5in (125.7cm) rear; trning circle 36ft (11m); length 153.2in (389.1cm); width 65in (165.1cm). PERFORMANCE maximum speed 150mpg (241.4kph) approx. PRODUCTION 2.

As with the Dick Jacobs Midgets, the basis was the steel platform with an aluminium body conforming to the GT shape, with flared arches for racing tyres and wheels.

1968 MG 1300

Obediently joining in when the 1100 became the 1300, the MG variant had ten per cent more power, which raised its top speed to nearly 100mph. Radial-ply tyres were standardised, it dispensed with the 1100's strip speedometer and had closer ratio gears although there were still only four of them. The engine remained firmly A-series, with three main bearings and noisy transfer gears. Harmony in the specifications of Wolseley, Riley and MG 1300s meant they became almost indistinguishable from one another except that the MG was available only with two doors. It still had praiseworthy ride and handling, despite reservations about how the front tended to dive to the inside if the throttle was closed suddenly in mid-corner. The radial-ply tyres magnified road noise and among the qualitative problems that varied from car to car were obstructive gearshifts and sticky rack and pinion steering.

Economy was a little below average, top speed up and acceleration about par for the class. In 1965 a triumph of miniaturisation brought an automatic transmission, developed by Automotive Products (AP), which fitted into the sumps of Minis and 1100/1300s. It was a good deal less smooth than full-sized automatics, invariably noisy, and unfortunately seldom reliable. It also made the MG less lively, and increased consumption of fuel.

BODY saloon, 2 doors, 4 seats; weight 1847lb (838kg), 1936lb (879kg) automatic. ENGINE 4 cylinders; front, transverse; 70.6mm x 81.3mm, 1275cc; cr 9.75:1; 70bhp (52.2kW) @ 6000rpm; 54.9bhp (40.9kW)/l; 77lbft (103Nm) @ 3000rpm. ENGINE STRUCTURE pushrod ohv, chain-driven camshaft; cast iron cyl head, block; 2 SU HS2 1¼in carbs, SU electric fuel pump; centrifugal and vacuum ign; 3-bearing crank. TRANSMISSION front wheel drive; 7.125in sdp diaphragm spring clutch; 4-speed manual, all-synchromesh; helical gear final drive 3.65:1: option AP 4-speed auto with torque converter, final drive 3.76:1. CHASSIS DETAILS steel monocoque; independent suspension by interconnected Hydrolastic units and rubber-cone springs; transverse wishbone at front, trailing arms at rear with anti-toll bar and two torsion bars for pitch stiffness; Lockheed brakes, 8in (20.3cm) disc front 8in (20.3cm) drum rear, pressure limiting valve; Cam Gears rack and pinion; 8.5gal (38.6l) fuel tank; 145-12in radial ply Dunlop SP68 tyres 4.0in rim. DIMENSIONS wheelbase 93.5in (237.5cm); track 51.5in (130.8cm) front, 50.75in (128.9cm) rear; turning circle 32.5ft (9.9m); ground clearance 5.25in (13.3cm); lngth 146.75in (372.7cm); wdth 60.25in (153cm); height 53.25in (135.3cm) PERFORMANCE maximum speed 97mph (155.7kph), 93mph (149kph) auto; 16.8mph (27kph) @ 1000rpm, 16.3mph (26.2kph) auto @ 1000rpm; 0-60mph (96kph) 14.1sec, 14.3sec auto; 12kg/bhp (16.1kg/kW), 12.6kg/bhp (16.8kg/kW) auto; fuel consumption 30mpg (9.4l/100km), 27mpg (10.5l/100km) auto. PRICE £925 11s 8d (£925 58p), £1021 8s 4d (£1021 42p) PRODUCTION Mk I & II 26,240

Issigonis was not the first designer to put an engine east-west, yet he set a trend in the 1950s that was adopted by the world.

1969-1974 Midget Mk 3/4 GAN 4/5

Upheavals during the strained development of British Leyland blurred the transition of the Mark III (announced October 1966) into the Mark IV Midget (announced October 1969). Design and development was nominally moved to Abingdon, although more as a way of writing the Healey family out of the script than to impart decision-making to MG. The Sprite was withdrawn from export markets and the Healey name dropped. The last vestiges of the MG grille were swept away in a rash of corporate co-ordination, with Leyland "flying L" (sometimes disparagingly known as the flying plughole) symbols predominating. Trendy-looking cast alloy wheels, matt black sills and seat trim with narrow central panels and horizontal ribbing came in. The cast wheels were replaced with cheaper Rostyles, and the fleetingly popular matt black windscreen surround was dropped within a year. With customary Leyland ineptitude the rear wheel arches had been rounded instead of squared-off, but this turned out to weaken the press-work, which was crumpling in rear-end impacts, so this was also changed back. One of the more useful innovations under pressure from dissatisfied owners, was an increase in the size of the fuel tank. Fuel consumption had deteriorated as a result of exhaust emission controls and increased weight, which had reduced the car's effective range to well under 200miles (322km).

BODY sports, 2 doors, 2 seats; weight 1548lb (702kg). ENGINE 4 cylinders, in-line; front; 70.61mm x 81.28mm, 1275cc; compr 8.8:1 8.0 optional; 65bhp (48.5kW) @ 6000rpm; 60bhp (38kW)/l); 72lbft (97Nm) @ 3000rpm. ENGINE STRUCTURE pushrod ohv, chain-driven camshaft; cast iron cylinder head, block; 2 SU HS2 1¼in carburettors, SU electric fuel pump; 3-bearing crankshaft. TRANSMISSION rear wheel drive; 6½ in diaphragm spring sdp clutch; 4-speed manual gearbox, synchromesh; hypoid final drive 3.9:1. CHASSIS DETAILS steel platform chassis; ifs by coil springs and wishbones; live rear axle semi-elliptic 5-leaf springs, Armstrong lever arm hydraulic dampers; optional anti-roll bar; Lockheed hydraulic brakes 8¼in (21cm) disc front, 7in (17.8cm) drums rear; rack and pinion steering; 7gal (31.8l) fuel tank; 145-13 Michelin radial-ply tyres; cast alloy wheels, later Rostyle steel, wire wheels optional. DIMENSIONS wheelbase 80in (203.2cm); front track 46.5in (118.1cm) with Rostyles or 45.25in (114.9cm), rear 45in (114.3cm) with Rostyles, or 44.75in (113.7cm); turning circle 30.1ft (9.2m); ground clearance 5in (12.7cm); length 135.25in (346.1cm); width 53in (134.5cm); height 49.75in (126.4cm). PERFORMANCE maximum speed 94mph (151kph); 16.5mph (26.5kph) @ 1000rpm; 0-60mph (96kph) 14.1sec; 10.8kg/kW (14.5kg/kW); fuel consumption 29.6mpg (9.5l/100km). PRICE £915 14s 9d (£915 74p). PRODUCTION GAN 4 13,722, GAN 5 86,650, total 100,372.

Radial ply tyres were standard in 1972, the suspension was raised half an inch to meet American headlamp and bumper regulations, and an alternator replaced the dynamo.

1972 SSV1 Experimental safety vehicle

A novelty of the SSVI was the British Leyland Alcohol Simulation Test (BLAST) that set the driver a coloured lights test to determine sobriety.

Throughout the 1970s compliance with world safety and emission control regulations was a contentious issue. Increasing demands on engineering resources, research, and development changed the nature of the motor industry. Planned obsolescence and the annual round of facelifts had to go by the board, as serious studies were undertaken in order to keep pace with legislation.

Safety was a public relations issue, much as greenery would become in the 1990s and, determined to show it could keep abreast of developments, British Leyland Motor Corporation (BLMC) asked MG to create an Experimental Safety Vehicle (SSV1). In order to ingratiate itself and look good to opinion-formers in the press and elsewhere, this curiosity incorporated a number of untried features. They included a Lockheed anti-roll system that led to a deterioration in handling, run-flat tyres, low-level soft bumpers supposed to reduce pedestrian injuries, air-bags and passive seat belts. There was a big rear-view mirror in the roof and body box-sections were filled with polyurethane foam, apparently to increase their strength in an accident. Triumph engineers at BLMC were assigned to produce anti-lock brakes and self-levelling headlamps.

It was not all wishful showcasing, however. With commendable prescience MG developed an idea Lucas had tried with infra-red technology back in 1962. SSV1 had a radar cruise control that closed the throttle and applied the brakes when catching up too closely with a car ahead. Twenty years or so later it would all have to be re-invented along with working air bags and anti-lock brakes.

BODY coupe, 2 doors, 2 +2 seats.ENGINE 4 cylinders, in-line; front; 80.26mm x 88.9mm, 1798cc; compr 8.8:1; 95bhp (70.8kW) @ 5400rpm; 52.8bhp (39.4kW)/l; 110lbft (148Nm) @ 3000rpm. ENGINE STRUCTURE pushrod overhead valve; chain-driven camshaft; cast iron cylinder head and block; 2 SU inclined H4 carburettors, SU electrical fuel pump; centrifugal and vacuum ignition control; 5-bearing crankshaft; engine rubber-mounted; oil cooler. TRANSMISSION rear wheel drive; Borg & Beck 8in (20.3cm) diaphragm spring clutch; 4-speed manual gearbox, all-synchromesh; single-piece open prop shaft; Salisbury hypoid bevel final drive 3.91:1. CHASSIS DETAILS steel monocoque structure; ifs by coil springs and unequal wishbones; live axle with semi-elliptic springs, optional anti-roll bar; Armstrong lever arm dampers; Lockheed hydraulic brakes, front 10.75in (27.3cm) discs, rear 10in (25.4cm) drums; rack and helical pinion steering; 12gal (54.6l) fuel tank; Dunlop Road Speed 5.90 - 14 tyres; 4J rims. DIMENSIONS wheelbase 91in (231.1cm); track 49in (22.9cm) (124.5cm); turning circle 30.5ft (9.3m); ground clearance 4.25in (10.8cm); width 60in (152.4cm). PERFORMANCE 16.4mph (26.3kph) @ 1000rpm.PRODUCTION 1.

1973-1976 MGB GT V8

In 1969 former Mini racer Ken Costello of Farnborough fitted an MGB with an aluminium Oldsmobile V8. Costello recognised the strong (by modern standards probably over-engineered) structure of a body shell was well capable over coping with more power and speed. Rover had bought the rights for the same engine from GM for the Rover 3.5 and Range Rover, and his second conversion was of an MGB GT with one of the new British-made engines. Beyond an MGC 9½in clutch and a 3.07:1 back axle the modifications required were almost elementary and Costello Motor Engineering began making them in steady numbers.

Astonishingly, thanks to the low weight of the bigger engine, the complete car was 90lb (40.8kg) lighter than the standard MGB, and did nearly 130mph (208.7kph). Costello's request to British Leyland for a supply of engines was his undoing. If there was a market for an MGB V8, BL wanted it to itself. A works prototype was commissioned and production commenced, even though the output of engines at the time was scarcely enough for Rover and Land Rover alone. Supplies to Costello were constrained but it scarcely mattered. Ever resourceful, he simply obtained Oldsmobile or Buick cylinder blocks, of which there were plenty in America and Europe, and carried on as before making mainly GTs, but also some roadsters including his own personal car. The factory only made GTs and was unable to export them to the United States because the engine was not de-toxed under

Federal US rules. To make things worse, Costello's announcement of the model came within two months of the Arab-Israel war that brought the world an oil crisis. From a peak in October 1973 of 176, within a year the numbers had shrunk to 18. They recovered to 93 in April 1975 then stopped the following year once British Leyland production had gone ahead.

BODY coupe, 2 doors, 2+2 seats; weight 2387lb (1082.7kg). ENGINE 8 cylinders, 90deg V; front; 88.96mm x 71.1mm, 3528cc; compr 8.25:1; 137bhp (102.2kW) @ 5000rpm; 38.8bhp (29kW)/l; 193ftlb (259Nm) @ 2900rpm. ENGINE STRUCTURE pushrod overhead valve; hydraulic tappets; aluminium cylinder block and heads; two 1¾in SU HIF6 carburettors; SU electric fuel pump; 5-bearing crankshaft. TRANSMISSION rear wheel drive; Borg & Beck diaphragm spring sdp clutch; 4-speed manual synchromesh gearbox, Laycock LH overdrive 0.82:1 standard; hypoid bevel final drive 3.07:1. CHASSIS DETAILS steel monocoque structure; ifs by wishbones, coil springs, anti-roll bar and lever-type dampers; Live rear axle with semi-elliptic springs and lever-type dampers; 10.7in (17.8cm) disc front 10in (25.4cm) drum rear hydraulic servo brakes; rack and pinion steering; 12gal (54.6l) fuel tank; alloy and steel composite wheels, 175HR x 14 tyres 5J rims. DIMENSIONS wheelbase 91in (231.1cm); track 49in (22.9cm) (124.5cm); turning circle 34ft (10.4m); ground clearance 4.5in (11.4cm); length 154.7in (17.8cm) (392.9cm), 158.25in (402cm) from autumn 1974; width 60in (152.4cm); height 50in (127cm), 51in (129.5cm) from autumn 1974. PERFORMANCE maximum speed 125.3mph (201.7kph); 28.5mph (45.8kph) o/d top, 23.4mph (37.6kph) top @ 1000rpm; 0-60mph (96kph) 7.7sec; 7.9kg/bhp (10.6kg/kW); 19.8mpg (14.3l/100km). PRICE £2293.96 on announcement, £3317 in autumn 1976. PRODUCTION 2591.

1974-1979 Midget 1500 GAN6

Leyland was run for the most part by former Triumph executives, promoted often beyond their capacity and skill by Lord Stokes and his acolytes. So, with the old BMC A-series at the end of its useful life, it was scarcely surprising that the Spitfire engine found its way into the Midget. For the first time since the introduction of baulk-ring synchromesh in 1962, there was also a major revision to the gearbox. A new all-synchromesh unit evolved round the single-rail design of the Morris Marina with wider ratios; unfortunately it made the car under-geared. There was not much more power and the improved torque of the engine turned out to be absolutely necessary in view of the extra weight of the new bumpers. These were deemed indispensable to meet approaching US safety legislation although the "rubber" was really moulded urethane foam over a steel base, making a major contribution to the increased weight of 1850lb (839kg). This was substantially more than the safe, simple Mark 1 Sprite's 1400lb (635kg), and the front air intake was so restricted it caused overheating until changes were brought in.

The ride height was raised by an inch through alterations to the front cross-member mounting and decambering the rear springs. This had a profound effect on ride and handling, an undeserved fate for a popular and hitherto exquisitely balanced little car. In 1977 the specification included head restraints, inertia-reel safety belts and later on a radio console and 2-speed wipers. Cecil Kimber, with his distrust of hydraulics, would have welcomed the addition of a brake failure warning light.

BODY sports, 2 doors, 2 seats; weight 1774lb (805kg). ENGINE 4 cylinders, in-line; front; 73.7mm x 87.5mm, 1493cc; compr 9.0:1; 66bhp (49.2kW) @ 5500rpm; 44.2bhp (33kW)/l; 77lbft (103Nm) @ 3000rpm. ENGINE STRUCTURE pushrod overhead valve, chain-driven camshaft; cast iron cylinder head, block; 2 SU HS4 1½ in carburettors, SU mechanical fuel pump; 3-bearing crankshaft. TRANSMISSION rear wheel drive; 7¼ in diaphragm spring sdp clutch; 4-speed manual gearbox, all-synchromesh; hypoid final drive 3.9:1. CHASSIS DETAILS steel platform chassis; ifs by coil springs and wishbones; live rear axle semi-elliptic 6-leaf springs, Armstrong lever arm hydraulic dampers; optional anti-roll bar; Lockheed hydraulic brakes 8¼in (21cm) disc front, 7in (17.8cm) drums rear; rack and pinion steering; 7gal (31.8l) fuel tank; 145-13 Michelin radial-ply tyres; Rostyle steel wheels, wire wheels optional. DIMENSIONS wheelbase 80in (203.2cm); track 46.3in (118cm) with Rostyles or 45.25in (114.9cm) front, 45in (114.3cm) with Rostyles or 44.75in (113.7cm) rear; turning circle 30.1ft (9.2m); ground clearance 3.25in (8.25cm); length 141in (358.1cm); width 60.25in (153cm); height 48.25in (122.6cm). PERFORMANCE maximum speed 101mph (163kph); 16.5mph (26.5kph) @ 1000rpm; 0-60mph (96kph) 12.3sec; 12.2kg/bhp (16.4kg/kW); fuel consumption 27.9mpg (10.1l/100km). PRICE £1,418.04. PRODUCTION 72,185.

1975–1980 MGB

In a despairing effort to meet increasingly severe American safety regulations, the MGB, like the Midget, was also equipped with energy absorbing bumpers. Heavy reinforcement lay behind them, the car's weight went up by 70lb (31.8kg), length by 5in (12.7cm) and further emission controls diminished engine power. Another increase in the camber of the rear springs added 1.5in (3.8cm) to the ride height and there was more packing in the front suspension to bring the bumpers up to an American minimum. The result, predictably, was a disaster. Additional weight induced more body roll, so it became necessary to fit an anti-roll bar at the rear as well as thickening the one at the front. The car felt lugubrious and its appearance suffered. Nobody believed the explanations by Leyland spin doctors who blamed legislators and safety authorities. In fact the management was failing to address the underlying problem, which was chronic under-investment in one of the smallest factories in the group's research and development programme.

Given the will and confidence in the future of the sports car market that was now handed to the likes of Datsun-Nissan and Mazda in Japan, better solutions to the problems could easily have been found. The US market modifications were so far-reaching and fundamental that there was no longer any practical way to separate home and export production and British Leyland lost confidence in the entire operation. Accordingly the massive bumpers and nearly all the US-market ancillaries, save the automatic seat belts and asthmatic Stromberg carburettor with associated emission control plumbing, were incorporated for the domestic market as well. Unsurprisingly MGB sales dropped by 10,000 a year, and although down to 24,576 in 1975, astonishingly recovered to 29,558 in 1976.

Manufactured by Marley Foam, from Bayflex 90 polyurethane, the bumpers were required to withstand a 5mph impact without deforming.

BODY coupe, 2 doors, 2+2 seats; weight 2781lb (1095kg). Roadster, 2 seats, 2304lb (1045kg). ENGINE 4 cylinders, in-line; front; 80.26mm x 88.9mm, 1798cc; compr 9.0:1; 84bhp (62.6kW) @ 5500rpm; 46.7bhp (34.8kW)/l; 105lbft (142Nm) @ 2500rpm. ENGINE STRUCTURE pushrod overhead valve; chain-driven camshaft; cast iron cylinder head and block; 2 SU inclined HIF4 carburettors, SU electrical fuel pump; centrifugal and vacuum ignition control; 5-bearing crankshaft; engine rubber-mounted; oil cooler. TRANSMISSION rwd; Borg & Beck 8in (20.3cm) diaphragm spring clutch; 4-speed manual gearbox, all-synchromesh; single-piece open prop shaft; hypoid bevel final drive 3.91:1. CHASSIS DETAILS steel monocoque structure; ifs by coil springs and unequal wishbones; live axle with semi-elliptic springs, anti-roll bars front (increased in size 1977) and rear; Armstrong lever arm dampers; Lockheed hydraulic brakes with vacuum servo, front 10.75in (27.3cm) discs, rear 10in (25.4cm) drums; rack and pinion steering; 11gal (50l) fuel tank; Pirelli Cinturato 165SR -14 tyres; 5J rims, wire wheels optional. DIMENSIONS wheelbase 91in (231.1cm); track 49.5in (125.7cm); turning circle 32ft (9.75m); ground clearance 4.19in (22.9cm) (11cm); length 158.25In (402cm); width 60in (152.4cm); height 49.25In (125.1cm). PERFORMANCE maximum speed 99mph (158.9kph); 17.9mph (28.7kph), 21.8mph (35kph) o/d top @ 1000rpm; 0-60mph (96kph) 14.0sec; 13kg/bhp (17.5kg/kW) coupe, 12.4kg/bhp (16.7kg/kW) roadster; fuel consumption 27.0mpg (10.5l/100km). PRICE £2,539. PRODUCTION 513,276 all MGB.

1975 MGB GT Anniversary

With an enthusiasm that overcame consideration for the finer points of history, 750 specially prepared MGB GTs celebrated what British Leyland's creaking and really quite cynical publicity machine decided was 50 years' production of MGs. Company history had become so equivocal that it depended on the definition of "MG" and "production". The limited edition anniversary cars incorporated a number of overdue and useful developments, such as replacement of the two six-volt batteries behind the seats with one 12-volt. The steering ratio was changed from 3½ turns lock to lock to 3 and the dashboard altered to include, rather belatedly since MGB drivers had been complaining about it since 1962, a new glove-locker lock. The switch for the new overdrive was moved to the gear lever.

MGB GT body shells had been re-engineered for the now discontinued V8, so they had a cross-flow radiator and thermostatically controlled electric cooling fan, which made up for a few of the horse power lost through emission control equipment. Wheels were the V8 cast alloy and steel pattern with 175 section tyres. Halogen headlights, tinted windows and head restraints were all standard, and the cars were all painted British Racing Green with a gold side-stripe and commemorative badge. A certificate and dashboard plaque detailing the production number from the commemorative run completed the ensemble.

BODY coupe; 2-doors; 2+2-seats; weight 2781lb (1095kg). ENGINE 4 cylinders, in-line; front; 80.26mm x 88.9mm, 1798cc; compr 9.0:1; 84bhp (62.6kW) @ 5500rpm; 46.7bhp (34.8kW)/l; 105lbft (142Nm) @ 2500rpm. ENGINE STRUCTURE pushrod ohv; chain-driven camshaft; cast iron cylinder head and block; 2 SU inclined HIF4 carburettors, SU electrical fuel pump; centrifugal and vacuum ignition control; 5-bearing crankshaft; engine rubber-mounted; oil cooler. TRANSMISSION rear wheel drive; Borg & Beck 8in (20.3cm) diaphragm spring clutch; 4-speed manual gearbox, all-synchromesh; single-piece open prop shaft; hypoid bevel final drive 3.91:1. CHASSIS steel monocoque structure; ifs by coil springs and unequal wishbones; live axle with semi-elliptic springs, anti-roll bars front and rear; Armstrong lever arm dampers; Lockheed hydraulic brakes, front 10.75in (27.3cm) discs, rear 10in (25.4cm) drums; rack and pinion steering; 11gal (50l) fuel tank; Pirelli Cinturato 175SR -14 tyres; 5J rims, wire wheels optional. DIMENSIONS wheelbase 91in (231.1cm); track 49.5in (125.7cm); turning circle 32ft (9.75m); ground clearance 4.19in (22.9cm) (11cm); length 158.25In (402cm); width 60in (152.4cm); height 49.25In (125.1cm). PERFORMANCE max speed 99mph (158.9kph); 17.9mph (28.7kph) @ 1000rpm, 21.8mph (35kph) o/d top; 0-60mph (96kph)14.0sec; 13kg/bhp (17.5kg/kW); fuel consumption 27.0mpg (10.5l/100km). PRICE £2,669. PRODUCTION 750.

1980 MGB Limited Edition roadster and GT

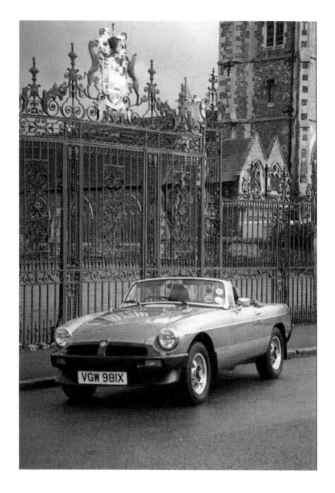

Even after closing off production at its Speke factory, BL still suffered from over-capacity and deemed Abingdon surplus to requirements. The irony of the announcement on 10 September 1979, soon after celebrations of 50 years of MG production in what had been the county town of rural Berkshire (changed in 1974 to Vale of the White Horse district of Oxfordshire), was not lost on generations of MG enthusiasts. It also followed closure of AEC at Park Royal and the end of car manufacturing at an old-established Standard Motor Company plant in Canley. John Thornley urged all the company's American dealers to get BL to reconsider, but to no avail, with the Corporation's creative accountants obstinately claiming a loss of £900 on every MGB. MG clubs mounted a protest rally but Sir Michael Edwardes pointed out that his preoccupation was with 100,000 jobs in BL as a whole, rather than 1,100 at strike-free Abingdon. Still, mindful of opportunities for profit, BL made a special edition of the last 1000 MGBs.

The production run had a chin spoiler, with roadsters finished in metallic bronze and gold LE stripes, GTs in pewter metallic with silver stripes. Orange and brown striped cloth upholstery completed the ensemble on roadsters; GTs had a silver grey interior. MGB power output for the UK increased to as much as 97bhp (72.3kW) but a Limited Edition roadster, finished in black, was also sold in America and although not as breathless as the 65bhp (48.5kW) Zenith-Stromberg cars of the mid-1970s, had smaller valves, one carburettor and was strangled with emission controls.

BODY coupe, 2 doors, 2+2 seats, weight 2781lb (1095kg). Roadster, 2 seats, 2304lb (1045kg). ENGINE 4 cylinders, in-line; front; 80.26mm x 88.9mm, 1798cc; compr: 9.0:1; 90bhp (67.1kW) @ 5500rpm; 50.1bhp (37.3kW)/l; 105lbft (142Nm) @ 2500rpm. ENGINE STRUCTURE pushrod ohv; chain-driven camshaft; cast iron cylinder head and block; 2 SU inclined HIF4 carbs, SU electrical fuel pump; centrifugal and vacuum ignition control; 5-bearing crank; engine rubber-mounted; oil cooler. TRANSMISSION rear wheel drive; Borg & Beck 8in (20.3cm) diaphragm spring clutch; 4-speed manual gearbox, all-synchromesh; single-piece open prop shaft; hypoid bevel final drive 3.91:1. CHASSIS DETAILS steel monocoque structure; ifs by coil springs and unequal wishbones; live axle with semi-elliptic springs, anti-roll bars front and rear; Armstrong lever arm dampers; Lockheed hydraulic brakes, front 10.75in (27.3cm) discs, rear 10in (25.4cm) drums; rack and pinion steering; 11gal (50l)) fuel tank; Pirelli Cinturato 175SR -14 tyres, 185-70 optional; 5J rims, wire wheels optional. DIMENSIONS wheelbase 91in (231.1cm); track 49.5in (125.7cm); turning circle 32ft (9.75m); ground clearance 4.19in (22.9cm) (11cm); length 158.25In (402cm); width 60in (152.4cm); height 49.25In (125.1cm). PERFORMANCE maximum speed 105mph (168.6kph); 17.9mph (28.7kph), 21.8mph (35kph) o/d top; 0-60mph (96kph) 14.0sec; 12.2kg/bhp (16.3kg/kW) coupe, 11.6kg/bhp (15.6kg/kW) roadster; fuel consumption 27mpg (10.5l/100km). PRICE £6,108 roadster, £6,376 GT. PRODUCTION 420 roadsters, 580 GTs.

Stag-pattern alloy wheels, an option since 1977, were standard but roadster buyers could specify wire wheels.

208 of them did so.

1980 MG Aston Martin proposal

By way of demonstrating its ambitions, the takeover consortium determined to save MG had a prototype Aston Martin MG built at Newport Pagnell. Aston Martin managing director Alan Curtis's instructions to designer William Towns was to use as much of the existing MGB as possible, but enhance its appeal in Continental Europe, America and Japan, which was emerging as a market where MGs were becoming firm favourites.

The aim was to keep production up to the current 600 a week, use the O-series engine (with an unspecified V6 later as an option), and Rover 3500 gearbox and back axle under licence from BL. Towns drew on the experience of BL's American subsidiary to gauge the market, and a standard MGB coupe was delivered to Aston Martin at Newport Pagnell as the basis for the facelift. The plan was to use it as a platform for a new range that included a Midget, and the B prototype, built inside a week, was intended to convince the government and backers to take the project seriously. Towns raised the windscreen, tidied up the BL safety bumpers and improved the cosmetics inside. It scarcely mattered that there was no time to engineer a fuel filler flap; the project was stillborn and Towns' renderings of a family of MGs were consigned to the realm of romantic might-have-beens.

BODY roadster; 2 doors, 2 seats approx 2304lb (1045kg). ENGINE 4 cylinders, in-line; front; 80.26mm x 88.9mm, 1798cc; compr 8.8:1; 95bhp (70.8kW) @ 5400rpm; 52.8bhp (39.4kW)/l; 110lbft (149Nm) @ 3000rpm. ENGINE STRUCTURE pushrod ohv; chain-driven camshaft; cast iron cylinder head and block; 2 SU inclined H4 carburettors, SU electrical fuel pump; centrifugal and vacuum ign control; 5-bearing crankshaft; engine rubber-mounted; oil cooler. TRANSMISSION rear wheel drive; Borg & Beck 8in (20.3cm) diaphragm spring clutch; 4-speed manual gearbox, all-synchromesh; single-piece open prop shaft; Salisbury hypoid bevel final drive 3.91:1. CHASSIS steel monocoque structure; ifs by coil springs and unequal wishbones; live axle with semi-elliptic springs, optional anti-roll bar; Armstrong lever arm dampers; Lockheed hydraulic brakes, front 10.75in (27.3cm) discs, rear 10in (25.4cm) drums; rack and helical pinion steering; 12gal (54.6l) fuel tank; Dunlop Road Speed 5.90 - 14 tyres; 4J rims; wire wheels optional. DIMENSIONS wheelbase 91in (231.1cm); track 49in (22.9cm) (124.5cm); turning circle 30.5ft (9.23m); ground clearance 4.25in (10.8cm); length 153.75in (390.5cm); width 60in (152.4cm); height 49.25in (125cm). PERFORMANCE maximum speed 108.1mph (173.5kph); 16.4mph (26.3kph) @ 1000rpm; 0-60mph (96kph) 12.1sec; fuel consumption 23.0mpg (12.3l/100km). PRODUCTION 1.

1982–1990 MG Metro 1300

Even when MG reappeared on a production car, some surviving new unregistered MGBs were still on sale. BL was reorganising itself as Austin-Rover, so in May 1962 applied MG to a supposedly sporting version of the economy Metro. It was by way of introduction to a turbocharged MG Metro due at the motor show in the autumn. This was the first genuine 100mph Metro and, true to their new-found trendiness, its designers given the job of applying MG identity were liberal with appliqué octagons and red piping on the upholstery. More to the point, they replaced steel wheels with ventilated alloy ones shod with low-profile tyres. A plastic surround to the rear window was claimed to produce a drag coefficient reduction of two decimal places, or not very much. An additional 12bhp (8.9kW) was extracted from the venerable A-series engine, now termed optimistically A-Plus, by means of extensive modifications including a new cam profile that gave more overlap and was even more extreme than the old Mini Cooper S. The compression ratio was raised from 9.4 to 10.5:1 by reducing combustion chamber volume and the size of cavities in the short-skirt pistons. Traditionally, MG engines had twin carburettors but this Metro had one with clever detailing in a water-heated inlet manifold to stabilise temperature of the ingoing mixture. The MG Metro was not quite in the Mini-Cooper class, yet achieved a moderate turn of speed with a good deal less fuss.

BODY saloon, 2 doors, 4 seats; weight 1785lb (811kg). ENGINE 4 cylinders; front, transverse; 70.61mm x 81.28mm, 1275cc; compr 10.5:1; 72bhp (53.7kW) @ 6000rpm; 56.5bhp (42.1kW)/l; 73lbft (98Nm) @ 4000rpm. ENGINE STRUCTURE pushrod ohv; chain-driven camshaft; cast iron cylinder block and head; SU HIF44 carburettor; contact-breaker ign; electric fan; 3-bearing crank. TRANSMISSION front wheel drive; sdp 7.13in clutch; 4-speed manual synchromesh gearbox; helical spur final drive 3.4441:1. CHASSIS steel monocoque structure; independent front suspension by wishbones and Hydragas springs, telescopic dampers; independent rear suspension by trailing arms and Hydragas units w integral damping; dual circuit brakes disc front 8.4in (21.3cm), rear 7in (17.8cm) drums, vacuum servo; rack and pinion steering; 7gal (32l) fuel tank; 155/70SR-12 radial-ply tyres, 5in rims. DIMENSIONS wheelbase 88.6in (225cm); track 50.2in (127.4cm); turning circle 34.1ft (10.4m) L, 32.25ft (9.9m) R; ground clearance 6.5in (16.5cm); length 134.1in (340.4cm); width 60.9in (22.9cm) (154.7cm); height 53.6in (135.9cm). PERFORMANCE maximum speed 103mph (166kph); 17.2mph (27.6kph) @ 1000rpm; 0-60mph (96kph) 10.9sec; 11.3kg/bhp (15.1kg/kW); fuel consumption 38.3mpg (7.3l/100km). PRICE £4,799. PRODUCTION 120,197.

1983-1990 MG Metro Turbo

Turbo Technics, a British tuning firm, produced the first turbocharged A-series in 1982 but Austin Rover, with Lotus Engineering as consultants, was not far behind. A turbocharger was duly strapped on, producing the most powerful production A-series ever. Its 93bhp (69.4kW) at 6130rpm was well over three times the output of the original A30, and 21 per cent more than the 1275S Mini-Cooper. Although a Garrett AiResearch T3 turbocharger blowing at 7.5psi (0.52kg-cm) straight through an SU carburettor sounded fairly rough and ready, more modern technology was on hand. Ducellier contactless ignition was an important step forward in electronic engine management.

Fifty years to the month after the supercharged 1100cc MG K3 Magnette was planned for racing, the MG Metro Turbo gave a good account of itself, not quite the earlier car's 110.4bhp (82.3kW)/l but not inadequate for a road car.

The MG Metro Turbo only ceased production when all Metros were rebadged as Rover 100s. It was perhaps not the most refined small hot hatch, with quite a lot of fore and aft movement of the transverse engine even on its new mountings. Still, power delivery was more progressive than many turbos of the day. The chief shortcoming was low gearing; there was no space in the gearbox for a fifth. It was only at high speeds that the extra power went to the edge of the Metro's handling and roadholding envelope.

BODY saloon, 2 doors, 4 seats; weight 1826lb (828kg). ENGINE 4 cylinders; front, transverse; 70.61mm x 81.28mm, 1275cc; compr 9.4:1; 93bhp (69.4kW) @ 6130rpm; 72.9bhp (54.4kW)/l; 85lbft (114Nm) @ 4000rpm. ENGINE STRUCTURE pushrod ohv; chain-driven cam; cast iron cyl block & head; Garret AiResearch T3 turbocharger, 7.5psi (.517bar) boost, SU HIF44 carb; Ducellier breakerless ignition; electric fan; 3-bearing crank.TRANSMISSION front wheel drive; sdp 7.13in clutch; 4-speed manual synchromesh gearbox; helical spur final drive 3.21:1. CHASSIS steel monocoque structure; ifs by wishbones and Hydragas springs, telescopic dampers; irs by trailing arms and Hydragas units with integral damping; dual circuit brakes disc front 8.4in, rear 7in (17.8cm) drums, vacuum servo; rack and pinion steering; 7gal (32l) fuel tank; 165/60SR-12 radial-ply tyres 5½in rims. DIMENSIONS wheelbase 88.6in (225cm); track 50.2in (127.4cm); turning circle 34.1ft (10.4m) L, 32.25ft (9.9m) R; ground clearance 6.5in (16.5cm); length 134.1in (340.4cm); width 60.9in (22.9cm) (154.7cm); height 53.6in (135.9cm). PERFORMANCE maximum speed 112mph (180.2kph); 18.6mph (29.9kph) @ 1000rpm; 0-60mph (96kph) 9.4sec; 8.9kg/bhp (11.9kg/kW); 30.3mpg (9.3l/100km). PRICE £5,650. PRODUCTION 21,968.

1983-1984 MG Maestro 1600

The first MG Maestro had the Austin-Rover R-series engine with a chain-driven overhead camshaft, two Weber carburettors and a short eight-port inlet manifold. It had breakerless electronic ignition to meet emission control endurance tests, and unleaded fuel.

A versatile car, with back seats that folded flat asymmetrically, it had a good level ride. Austin-Rover abandoned the interconnected Hydrolastic and Hydragas of the unlamented Allegro in favour of coil springs. Among its innovations was an electronic facia with solid state vacuum fluorescent displays and a voice synthesiser, neither of which caught on. The Volkswagen-derived 5-speed gearbox had close ratios and a high final drive that made fifth an overdrive at 0.91:1. It was a heavy car with some serious shortcomings that included difficult hot starting, drive-line shunt and poor fuel economy. Austin-Rover's quality problems were exacerbated by a shortage of time and parsimony over the development of new cars so the Maestro suffered accordingly.

After only 17 months the R-series was replaced in the Austin Maestro by the S-series, with a toothed belt drive to the camshaft. The cylinder head was turned through 180deg so that the inlet side faced the bulkhead. MG followed suit when the S-series was also installed in its version but not many were made before the opportunity came to set it quietly aside.

Data for R-series:

BODY saloon, 5 doors, 4 seats; weight 2190 lb (993kg). ENGINE 4 cylinders; front, transverse; 76.2mm x 87.6mm, 1598cc; compr 9.7:1; 103bhp (76.8kW) @ 6000rpm; 64.5bhp (48.1kW)/l; 100lbft (134Nm) @ 4000rpm. ENGINE STRUCTURE chain-driven ohv; cast iron cylinder block and head; twin dual fixed-choke downdraught Weber 40DCNF carburettors; breakerless electronic ignition; electric fan; 5-bearing crank.

TRANSMISSION front wheel drive; sdp 7.9in (22.9cm) clutch; 4-speed manual synchromesh gearbox; helical spur final drive 3.65:1. CHASSIS steel monocoque structure; ifs by strut and lower arm, coil springs, telescopic dampers and anti-toll bar. Semi-independent rear by trailing arms, torsion beam, coil springs telescopic dampers and anti-roll bar; hydraulic servo diagonally split circuit brakes 9.5in (24.1cm) discs, 8.0in (20.3cm) drums; rack and pinion steering; 11.7gal (53l) fuel tank; P8 radial ply 175/65SR tyres 5½in rims, aluminium alloy wheels.

DIMENSIONS wheelbase 98.7in (17.8cm) (250.7cm); track front 59in (22.9cm) (149.9cm), rear 58in (20.3cm) (147.3cm); turning circle 35ft (10.7m); ground clearance 5.8in (20.3cm) (14.7cm); length 159.5in (405cm); width 66.4in (168.7cm); height 56.3in (142.9cm). PERFORMANCE maximum speed 111mph (179kph); 19.9mph (31.9kph) @ 1000rpm; 0-60mph (96kph) 9.6sec; 9.6kg/bhp (12.9kg/kW); 26.8mpg (10.5l/100km).

PRICE £6245. PRODUCTION 12,427 R-series, 2,762 S-series.

1984 MG Metro 6R4

Built under rules changed prematurely for the sake of safety, club rally drivers could buy 6R4s with 250bhp (186.4kW). Works cars could have up to 380bhp (283.4kW). The 1984 prototype had been under development for three years by Frank Williams Grand Prix Eznginering to a design by Patrick Head, but its resemblance to a Metro was superficial.

Its mid-engine was a V6 cut down from a Rover V8 and its four-wheel drive enabled it to compete with Audi Quattro, Peugeot 205 and Lancia Delta. The engine evolved as a highly original Austin-Rover design by David Wood. Cosworth Engineering cast new blocks and heads and electronic engine management was by Lucas Micos, a research and development offshoot of Lucas. Ferguson technology was incorporated in the four wheel drive system, with a propeller shaft to the right of the engine, and strut suspension was adopted to distribute chassis loads more widely.

Had Group B (for which it was designed) continued, the 6R4 would probably have been successful, its light weight and low inertia having proved convincing to both enthusiastic Austin Rover Group (ARG) motor sport chief John Davenport as well as its drivers.

The engine found an unexpected lease of life when Tom Walkinshaw acquired rights to it for the Jaguar XJR-10. As the JRV-6 with two turbochargers in the Jaguar it took part in 26 races in 1989-1991, winning six of them.

BODY saloon, 2 doors, 2 seats; weight 2266lb (1030kg).ENGINE 6 cylinders, 90 deg V; mid, lengthwise; 92mm x 75mm, 2991cc; compr 12.0:1; 410bhp (305.7kW) @ 9000rpm; 137.1bhp (102.2kW)/l; 270lbft (362Nm) @ 6500rpm. ENGINE STRUCTURE two belt-driven overhead camshafts per bank; 4 valves per cylinder; Mahle slipper pistons, dry liners; aluminium cylinder heads and block; Lucas Micos mapped electronic ignition and 6-point fuel injection; 4-bearing crank; rally version machined from solid En40b, Club version forged; dry sump. TRANSMISSION four wheel drive; Borg & Beck twin plate diaphragm spring clutch; 5-speed manual dog-engaged gearbox, synchromesh on Club; spiral bevel final drive, interchangeable ratios; epicyclic torque-splitting differential, viscous coupling.CHASSIS DETAILS space-frame tubular steel and aluminium structure; integral roll cage; body aluminium, carbon fibre-reinforced grp; ifs and irs by coil springs, struts, Bilstein telescopic dampers anti-roll bar, all fully adjustable; adjustable ratio split dual circuit 12in (30.5cm) ventilated disc brakes; rack and pinion steering centre take-off; two 13.2gal (60l) fuel tanks; various competition tyres, Dymag cast mag alloy wheels. DIMENSIONS wheelbase 94.1in (239.1cm); track front 59.45in (151cm), rear 59.7in (151.5cm); length 131.9in (335cm); width 74in (188cm); height 59.1in (150cm) depending on suspension level. PERFORMANCE maximum speed 155mph (248.8kph); 0-60mph (96kph) 4.3sec; 2.5kg/bhp (3.4kg/kW). PRICE £40,000. PRODUCTION more than 200.

1984-1991 MG Montego 2.0EFi

The Montego was effectively a three-box version of the Maestro, and slightly more distinguished. The wheelbase was 2.3in (5.8cm) longer and common body parts were the front bulkhead, floorpan, inner front wings and bits of the doors. A roomy car with a big boot, from 1984 Austin versions had S-series engines, but the MG had the O-series 2.0litre with a slightly rudimentary (compared with sophisticated successors) fuel injection system developed jointly by Austin-Rover and Lucas. This measured intake airflow, by means of the electrical resistance of a heated wire for regulating fuel to the cylinders. It worked in conjunction with electronic transistorised ignition along the lines of Bosch Motronic, which mapped load, speed and temperature.

MG was being thrust into the new age of engine management while Austin and Vanden Plas Montegos laboured with carburettors. The Vanden Plas was the best-equipped and had as standard the power-assisted steering that cost an extra £285 on the MG.

Meanwhile the management of what was now called Austin Rover Group (ARG) in its clumsy corporate way, decreed that MGs, besides a sprinkling of octagons, would be distinguished by red stripes in the bumpers, red seat belts, red graphics on the instruments and red trim on the upholstery.

The Montego was lively, well-equipped and rode comfortably, but it was still neither quiet nor refined enough, or indeed sufficiently well made to match opposition from the likes of BMW.

BODY saloon, 4 doors, 5 seats; weight 2300lb (1043kg). ENGINE 4 cylinders; front, transverse; 84.5mm x 89.0mm, 1994cc; compr 9.0:1; 115bhp (85.8kW) @ 5500rpm; 57.7bhp (43kW)/l; 134lbft (180Nm) @ 2800rpm. ENGINE STRUCTURE belt-driven overhead camshaft; cast iron block, aluminium cylinder head, block; electronic breakerless ignition, Lucas L-type fuel injection; 5-bearing crank.TRANSMISSION front wheel drive; sdp diaphragm spring clutch; 5-speed manual all synchromesh gearbox; helical spur final drive 3.875:1. CHASSIS steel monocoque structure; ifs by struts and lower arms, coil springs, telescopic dampers, anti-roll bar; semi-independent rear, trailing arms, torsion beam, coil springs, telescopic dampers; dual circuit servo brakes, 9.5in (24.1cm) ventilated discs, 8in (20.3cm) drums rear; rack and pinion, PAS opt; 11gal (50l) fuel tank; Dunlop TD SP Sport 180/65HR-365 tyres 5in rims, aluminium alloy wheels. DIMENSIONS wheelbase 101in (256.5cm); track front 56.7in (144cm), rear 57.4in (145.8cm); turning circle 34.1ft (10.4m) L, 35.75ft (10.9m) R; ground clearance 6.2in (15.7cm); length 175.9in (446.8cm); width 67.3in (171cm); height 55.9in (142cm). PERFORMANCE maximum speed 114mph (183kph); 20.6mph (33kph) @ 1000rpm; 0-60mph (96kph) 8.9sec; 9.1kg/bhp (12.2kg/kW); fuel consumption 29.3mpg (9.6l/100km). PRICE £8,165.20. PRODUCTION 34,476.

1984-1991 MG Maestro 2.0 EFi

In October 1984 the 2.0litre, belt-driven, overhead camshaft fuel injected O-series engine replaced the ill-starred 1600, and a Honda gearbox purloined from the joint ARG-Honda project XX (sometimes in the acrimony following the split known as "Double-Cross") replaced the Volkswagen one. The result, as at least one dealer put it, "…was what the car should have been in the first place." Power and torque were enhanced and the performance was now more of a match for opposition such as the Golf GTi and the Astra GTE. A digital dashboard was now an option; the Maestro's instruments were once again analogue and there were some exterior enhancements such as a body colour grille and bumpers. Although refinement was never a feature of the O-series on start-up, at least it did usually start up, whether warm or cold, which was more than could be said for its predecessor. The 2.0litre also scored on fuel consumption, with a 7mpg (40.4l/100km) improvement on the 1600. The standard steering was too low-geared for a sporty car but a higher geared power assisted option was available. ARG was catching up with modern technology. The O-series engine management system from the Montego incorporated Lucas L-type multi-point fuel injection and electronic ignition with knock sensing.

BODY saloon, 5 doors, 4 seats; weight 2150lb (975.2kg). ENGINE 4 cylinders; front, transverse; 84.5mm x 89.0mm, 1994cc; compr 9.1:1; 115bhp (85.8kW) @ 5500rpm; 57.7bhp (43kW)/l; 134lbft (180Nm) @ 2800rpm. ENGINE STRUCTURE chain-driven overhead camshaft; cast iron cylinder block and aluminium head; Lucas L-type fuel injection; breakerless electronic ignition; electric fan; 5-bearing crankshaft. TRANSMISSION front wheel drive; sdp diaphragm spring clutch; 5-speed manual synchromesh gearbox; helical spur final drive 3.93:1. CHASSIS steel monocoque structure; ifs by strut and lower arm, coil springs, telescopic dampers and anti-toll bar. Semi-independent rear by trailing arms, torsion beam, coil springs telescopic dampers and anti-roll bar; hydraulic vacuum servo diagonally split circuit brakes 9.5in (24.1cm) ventilated discs, (20.3cm) (20.3cm) drums; rack and pinion steering, optional PAS; 11gal (50l) fuel tank; MXV radial ply 175/65SR tyres, 5½in rims aluminium alloy wheels. DIMENSIONS wheelbase 98.7in (250.7cm); track front 59in (149.9cm); rear 58in (20.3cm) (147.3cm); turning circle 33ft 8in (20.3cm) (10.3m); ground clearance 5.8in (20.3cm) (14.7cm); length 159.5in (24.1cm) (404.9cm); width 66.4in (168.7cm); height 56.3in (142.9cm). PERFORMANCE maximum speed 115mph (185kph); 21.9mph (35.2kph) @ 1000rpm; 0-60mph (96kph) 8.5sec; 8.5kg/bhp (11.4kg/kW); fuel consumption 33.4mpg (8.5l/100km). PRICE £7,249. PRODUCTION 32,725.

Increasingly burdensome emission control regulations, demanding that engines
run for 50,000 miles and remain in tune without attention,
brought out the best in engineers.

1985–1991 MG Montego Turbo

"Old Number One" was pulled from retirement for Montego Turbo publicity picture.

It may have seemed logical to believe that, since the Montego EFi had been a modest success, adding 33bhp (24.6kW) to make it even faster would enhance it. However, the first examples in 1985 were less than exemplary. Turbo lag made them unruly, demanding a great deal of experience from a driver to handle. Not enough was known about torque steer in conjunction with the way turbo power was supplied at the time in sudden surges. Engineers had to adjust the turbo, which worked at incandescent temperatures and spun at the limits of materials' integrity, to reduce these to an acceptable level. There had never been front wheel drive cars with such abrupt uneven heaves occurring in arrears of a driver's plans.

In the wet it demanded deft handling. The trouble was not only that the extra 35lbft (46.9Nm) of extra torque arrived at 3500rpm instead of 2800rpm, but also the turbo breathed in through a solitary SU and so did not deliver power smoothly. It came in great floods and the engine also lost its tune quicker than it would have had with good (even though complicated and expensive) fuel injection.

In 1986 the front suspension was modified, steering rack lowered, gearing raised and the track control arms altered. Springs and dampers were already stiffer than the non-turbo but owners still complained about stability. In an effort to improve it, the front air dam was redesigned so that in the end the Montego Turbo was almost civilised. It was even quite good value at the lower end of the turbocharged price spectrum.

BODY saloon, 4 doors, 5 seats; weight 2380lb (1079.6kg). ENGINE 4 cylinders; front, transverse; 84.5mm x 89.0mm, 1994cc; compr 8.5:1; 150bhp (111.9kW) @ 5500rpm; 75.2bhp (56.1kW)/l; 169lbft (227Nm) @ 3500rpm. ENGINE STRUCTURE belt-driven overhead camshaft; sodium-filled exhaust valves; cast iron block, aluminium cylinder head; electronic breakerless electronic ignition; Garrett AiResearch T3 turbocharger and intercooler, 10psi (0.7bar) boost; ARG (SU-type) single variable choke carburettor; 5-bearing crankshaft. TRANSMISSION front wheel drive; sdp diaphragm spring clutch; 5-speed manual all synchromesh gearbox; helical spur final drive 3.647:1. CHASSIS steel monocoque structure; ifs by struts and lower arms, coil springs, telescopic dampers, anti-roll bar (+2mm); semi-independent rear, trailing arms, torsion beam, coil springs, anti-roll bar, telescopic dampers; dual circuit servo brakes, 9.5in (24.1cm) ventilated discs, 8in (20.3cm) drums rear; rack and pinion PAS; 11gal (50l) fuel tank; radial ply 190/65HR-365 tyres 5.3in rims, aluminium alloy wheels. DIMENSIONS wheelbase 101in (256.5cm); track front 56.7in (144cm), rear 57.4in (145.8cm); turning circle 35.1ft (10.7m) L, 35.75ft (10.9m) R; ground clearance 6.2in (15.7cm); length 175.9in (446.8cm); width 67.3in (171cm); height 55.9in (142cm). PERFORMANCE maximum speed 125mph (200.7kph); 25mph (40.1kph) @ 1000rp; 0-60mph (96kph) 7.5sec; 7.2kg/bhp (9.6kg/kW); fuel con 23.0mpg (12.3l/100km).PRICE £10,300.55. PRODUCTION 7,276.

1985 MG EX-E

EX-E was unveiled at the Frankfurt Motor Show, to astonished applause from the assembled European press, which had started to suppose British industry no longer capable of such flights of fancy. It was never accorded the praise it deserved, as a turning point for an industry widely regarded as in terminal decline following years of labour disputes and stagnation. Five years after the demise of Abingdon and the MGB, it was the first glimmer of hope that MG as a make in its own right might not be dead but, like the Monty Python parrot of 1969, only resting.

Austin Rover morale had been low until its vigorous chairman and chief executive Harold Musgrove installed Royden Axe, formerly of Rootes and Chrysler, as director of design in 1982. Roy Axe's Canley studio had two directors; Gordon Sked, responsible for exterior, and Richard Hamblin for interior design. Included in a number of projects was an open two-seater MG Midget based on the Metro and drawn up by another promising young designer, Gerry McGovern. The EX-E had glass reinforced plastic (grp) body panels by Specialised Mouldings, a Huntingdon firm associated with

Lola cars, on an aluminium frame built to a modular design by Gaydon Technology A Cd of 0.24 was claimed, and it also incorporated concept-car features of the mid-1980s such as a hands-free cellular phone and satellite navigation. There was talk of a production version of EX-E with a Rover M16 engine. It certainly had the makings of a road car, but such was the pressure to sustain the volume end of the business that neither the government nor British Aerospace, which bought Austin-Rover in 1988, were ever likely to put up the cash.

BODY coupe, 2 doors, 2 seats. ENGINE 6 cylinder, 90 deg V; mid, lengthwise; 92mm x 75mm, 2991cc; compression 12.0:1; 250bhp (186.4kW) @ 7000rpm; 83.6bhp (62.3kW)/l; 225lbft (302Nm) @ 6500rpm. ENGINE STRUCTURE two belt-driven overhead camshafts per bank; 4 valves per cylinder; Mahle slipper pistons, dry liners; aluminium cylinder heads and block; Lucas Micos mapped electronic ignition and 6-point fuel injection; 4-bearing forged crank; dry sump lubrication. TRANSMISSION four wheel drive; Borg & Beck twin plate diaphragm spring clutch; 5-speed synchromesh gearbox; spiral bevel final drive; epicyclic torque-splitting differential, viscous coupling. CHASSIS DETAILS space-frame tubular steel and aluminium structure; ifs and irs by double wishbones coil springs, telescopic dampers anti-roll bar; experimental ride-height selection; dual circuit 12in (30.5cm) ventilated disc brakes with ABS; rack and pinion steering centre take-off; 215/45VR17 tyres, cast al alloy 17in wheels, 7Jrims. PERFORMANCE maximum speed estimated 170mph (272.9kph); 0-60mph (96kph) estimated 5.0sec. PRODUCTION 1.

1989 MG DR2 (PR5) prototype

A meeting of minds between Richard Hamblin, Rover Director of Special Projects reporting to Marketing Director Kevin Morley (pictured over), Roy Axe of Design Research Associates, Gordon Sked in the Canley studio and Graham Day among others, led in 1989 to Project Phoenix.

This studied a number of initiatives and crucially, since Abingdon was long closed and there was no specific MG design office, to the recruitment of outsiders. Day approved a budget of £750,000 for three principal Phoenix Routes (codenamed PR) to pursue up to prototype builds. PR1 was assigned to Motor Panels' prototypes division to look at a front M16-engined front wheel drive car based broadly on a Maestro platform.

Reliant at Tamworth took on PR2, a front-engine rear-drive car on its Scimitar chassis with a Rover V8 engine driving the rear wheels. PR3 was a mid-engine rear wheel drive car with a K-series engine by Automotive Development Centre. Plastic bodywork, retro designs and other avenues were described by David Knowles, in his MGF study that details the entire family of four Phoenix prototypes secured by the British Motor Museum that claims the world's largest collection of

historic British cars. This includes PR5/DR2, drawn up by Austin-Healey enthusiast Royden Axe (1937–2010) aimed at an altogether larger car than the other Phoenix strategies. Like PR2, it had a Rover V8 engine driving the rear wheels but built on a TVR chassis and a 1991 assessment described it as in the Jaguar XJ-S market priced between £40,000 and £45,000 and comparable to the Rover 800 Coupe although well short of Porsche in technical merit or Honda NSX supercar status.

The Gaydon exhibit (picture on previous page) was consigned an interior straight out of the TVR donor car it was made from rather than the more luxurious design that Axe intended. Gaydon's plaque says:
'This design, eventually coded PR5, was a front runner during the design thinking for a new MG. It had a British feel and, at the same time, was big enough to appeal to the American market. It was Rover's less successful business in the United States however, which led to the project being retired and to the adoption of the more compact mid-engined design being carried forward to the MGF.'

1989–1991 MG Maestro Turbo

The last Austin Rover Group (ARG) saloon hopefully had the turbocharged Montego engine in the Maestro. It was a short-lived tour de force; although the fastest production MG to date at just under 130mph (208.7kph), it was less refined than its direct competitor, the Peugeot 309GTi. It was, however, £1000 cheaper with changes in appearance commissioned from Tickford coachbuilders in a bizarre return to a firm, which (like Salmons) had been making MG bodies on and off for well over 50 years. Tickford was emerging from Aston Martin ownership, making its own version of the MG Metro and completed the Maestros at its works in Bedworth, near Coventry.

ARG's attempts to improve handling of the Maestro/Montego pair without relying entirely on the experience of its customers in the field were showing some results. Spring rates, anti-roll bars and camber settings had all been revised and the latest gas-filled dampers contributed to behaviour that was tamed but still fell some way short of the competition. Low speed ride was turbulent and a problem remained with wheelspin in the lower gears coming out of corners. A limited slip differential might have improved matters, electronic anti-wheelspin measures were not yet widely available and, with price still the over-riding consideration in corporate thinking, they were disregarded.

It looked for a time as though the Maestro Turbo would be the last with an MG badge, as production was discontinued in anticipation of a new range of Rovers.

BODY saloon, 4 doors, 4 seats; weight 2379lb (1080kg). ENGINE 4 cylinders; front, transverse; 84.5mm x 89.0mm, 1994cc; cr 8.5:1; 152bhp (113.3kW) @ 5100rpm; 76.2bhp (56.8kW)/l; 169lbft (227Nm) @ 3500rpm. ENGINE STRUCTURE belt-driven overhead camshaft; sodium-filled exhaust valves; cast iron block, aluminium cylinder head; electronic breakerless electronic ignition; Garrett AiResearch T3 turbocharger and intercooler, 10psi (0.7bar) boost; ARG (SU-type) single variable choke carb; 5-bearing crank. TRANSMISSION front wheel drive; sdp diaphragm spring clutch; 5-speed manual all synchro gearbox; helical spur final drive 3.647:1. CHASSIS steel monocoque structure; ifs by strut and lower arm, coil springs and anti-roll bar. Semi independent rear by trailing arms, torsion beam, coil springs and anti-roll bar, Telescopic gas-filled dampers front and rear; hydraulic servo diagonally split circuit brakes 9.5in (24.1cm) ventilated discs, (20.3cm) drums; rack and pinion PAS; 11gal (53l) tank; MXV2 radial ply 185/55 VR15 tyres 6in rims, aluminium wheels. DIMENSIONS wheelbase 98.7in (250.7cm); track 58.3in (148cm) front, 57.3in (145.5cm) rear; turning circle 33.8ft (10.3m); ground clearance 7in (17.8cm); length 157.6in (400.3cm); width 76in (193cm) including mirrors; height 56.1in (14.2cm). PERFORMANCE maximum speed 129mph (208kph); 25mph (40.1kph) @ 1000rpm; 0-60mph (96kph) 6.9sec; 7.1kg/bhp (9.5kg/kW); 20.1mpg (14.1l/100km). PRICE £12,999.
PRODUCTION 501.

1992–1994 MG RV8

Modern management turned its back on the modesty of MG Midgets and masterpieces of 1930s like 1½ litre Rileys and Aston Martins. The culture of the 1990s prompted by the remanufacture of cars like ersatz Shelby Cobras tempted it to squeeze the biggest engine obtainable into remanufactured MGB bodyshells. This became the basis for a car with classic overtones, elegant furnishings and an exciting performance even though it fitted only obliquely into MG traditions.

Unlike 1980s Limited Editions that were essentially valedictory and sold slowly, the 2000 RV8 may have made gradual progress at first, but following its appearance at the Tokyo Motor Show was seized on with enthusiasm by Japanese buyers. It was soon commanding premium prices and the project never faltered thereafter.

The body was 25 per cent MGB, with floor pan, doors and boot lid carried over. Almost everything else was new; body sills, wings, bonnet and, effectively, all four corners. The huge wheels were alloy split rims with large-section tyres, which accounted for the heavy steering. The cockpit was

handsomely trimmed. The black-framed windscreen was the same shape as the old MGB, but inside the upholstery would have done credit to a Bentley. The wood and leather was sumptuous. If you were to paint a picture of the RV8 client, a 50-something who couldn't afford a decent MG when he was 25, now was his chance. He wanted to keep up with the traffic. He had become accustomed to wood and leather in his executive saloon and did not much want to give it up.

A thoroughbred for grand touring, driven circumspectly the fuel consumption was tolerable - just as well because nobody had thought about the size of the fuel tank. It had power to spare and a comfortable ride and flaws only showed if it was regarded as a modern sports car. The ride was good at slow speeds on well-surfaced roads but there was insufficient spring travel at the back to provide the compliance of more modern designs.

BODY roadster, 2 doors, 2 seats; weight 2822lb (1280kg). ENGINE 8 cylinders, 90deg V; front; 94mm x 71mm, 3946cc; compr 9.35:1; 187bhp (139.4kW) @ 4750rpm; 47.4bhp (35.3kW)/l; 231lbft (310Nm) @ 3200rpm. ENGINE STRUCTURE pushrod ohv; hydraulic tappets; aluminium cylinder block and heads; breakerless electronic ign, Lucas multi-point fuel injection; 5-brng crank. TRANSMISSION rwd; sdp clutch; 5-speed manual all synchromesh gearbox; final drive 3.31:1. CHASSIS steel monocoque structure; ifs by double wishbone and coil springs, telescopic dampers, anti-roll bar; live axle with control arms, tapered leaf semi-elliptic springs, telescopic dampers, anti-roll bar; hydraulic servo ventilated 10.6in (27cm) disc front brakes 11in (28cm) drums at rear; rack and pinion steering; 11gal (51l) fuel tank; 205-65VR tyres, 15in cast alloy wheels, 6J rims. DIMENSIONS wheelbase 92in (233cm); track front 49in (124.5cm), rear 52in (132cm); turning circle ft (m); ground clearance in (cm); length 158in (20.3cm) (401cm); width 67in (169.4cm); height 52in (132cm).PERFORMANCE maximum speed 135mph (216.7kph); 29mph (46.6kph) @ 1000rpm; 0-60mph (96kph) 5.9sec; 6.8kg/bhp (9.2kg/kW); fuel consumption 20.2mpg (14l/100km). PRICE £26,500. PRODUCTION 2000.

1995 MGF 1.8i

Mid-engined and up to date, although holding good to MG's founding principle of using major components from a volume series, Project Phoenix in the late 1980s gained momentum after 1990 when Mazda's MX-5 showed sports cars in MG's idiom could still be profitable. Design work began using Maestro components along with transverse twin overhead camshaft O-series engines and front wheel drive. There were two front-engined V8s, one steel, one with plastic body panels.

Rover and John Towers, director of engineering, had few illusions. Marketing director Kevin Morley thought badge engineering passé. Yet all recognised the necessity to continue with common modules, furthermore during ownership by British Aerospace strictures were in place that made it impossible to invest much cash. The partnership with Mayflower in body manufacture was crucial. Roy Axe's Design Research Associates at Warwick, Rover Group, Special products department under Don Wyatt and Nick Stephenson, head of engineering and design all set to work. In what remained of a former Triumph plant in Canley, the proposal by the MGA Developments design consultancy of Steve Harper created a design schemed for production by a Design Studio with Gerry McGovern given approval by Rover in 1992.

The 16-valve K-series engine had a unique aluminium sandwich structure, held together by ten through-bolts, beginning as a study into plastic engine components. It went on to research aluminium elements and emerged as one of the most innovative engine designs of the 1990s. Experimental cars did not look like MGFs. They included Toyota MR2s with K-series engines and 15 were Metro vans with the engine behind the driver. About 26 hand-made prototypes with production parts were road tested followed by another 34, and 165 Quality Proving (QP) cars ensured the design was ready for production. In all, 239 were made before production started in July 1995 under the new BMW regime.

BODY roadster, 2 doors, 2 seats; weight 2337lb (1060kg). ENGINE 4 cylinders; mid transverse; 80mm x 89.3mm, 1796cc; compr 10.5:1; 118bhp (88kW) @ 5500rpm; 65.7bhp (49kW)/l; 122lbft (165Nm) @ 3000rpm. ENGINE STRUCTURE twin belt-driven ohc; 16-valves; aluminium cam cover, cam carrier, cyl head & block, bearing ladder, sump, damp cylinder liners; MEMS electronic ign multi-point fuel injection; 5-bearing crank.
TRANSMISSION rwd; sdp clutch; 5-speed manual synchromesh; final drive 3.938:1.CHASSIS steel monocoque structure; ifs by double wishbones, interconnected Hydragas springs, anti-roll bars; servo ventilated front disc brakes, 9.5in (24.1cm), solid at rear; ABS optional; rack and pinion, electric PAS optional; 11gal (50l) fuel tank; 6-spoke alloy wheels; 185/55 VR15 tyres front, 205/50 VR15 rear; 6J rims. DIMENSIONS wheelbase 93.7in (238cm); track 55.1in (140cm) front, 55.5in (141cm) rear; turning circle 34.45ft (10.5m); ground clearance 47.2in (120cm); length 154.1in (391.4cm); width 64.1in (162.8cm); height with hood 49.6in (126cm). PERFORMANCE maximum speed 120mph (193kph); 22.1mph (35.5kph) @ 1000rpm; 0-60mph (96kph) 8.7sec; 9kg/bhp (12kg/kW); fuel con 26.4mpg (10.7l/100km). PRICE £15,995 PAS £550, ABS £650, hardtop £995: 1996 £16,395. PRODUCTION 77,296 all MG Rover MGF.

1995 MGF 1.8i VVC

The reception accorded the MGF was enthusiastic. It was oversubscribed as soon as it went on sale and commanded premium prices at auction. Critics praised the ride, the stiff body construction, refinement, brakes, grip, trim and appearance. The more expensive version with Variable Valve Control (VVC), described by some of its engineers as VVC – Very Very Complicated, provided an additional 25bhp (18.6kW) and took the engine up to over 7000rpm. A mechanical link controlled the cam lobes on the inlet side by an eccentric under the engine management system. This kept them open longer for more power but closed longer for more torque. Improving the performance by greater efficiency rather than merely gulping in more fuel made it as economical as the simpler version, putting the MGF among the leaders in an increasingly competitive class.

Reservations about anti-lock brakes and power steering being optional at extra cost did not apply to the VVC model because they were included in the price.

The handling was excellent for a touring car, a shade compliant for a sports car but, with a bias towards understeer, it was strictly in accordance with the well-established Safety Fast slogan. The entire concept demonstrated how well its designers had understood the MG market. The image of the make may have altered a lot during the dog days of British Leyland, but now that it seemed to be back in independent hands and was being run by car people rather than accountants, it seemed possible that MG could now restart, more or less, where it had left off in 1980.

BODY roadster, 2 doors, 2 seats; weight 2359lb (1070kg). ENGINE 4 cylinders; mid transverse; 80mm x 89mm, 1796cc; compr 10.5:1; 145bhp (108.1kW) @ 7000rpm; 80.7bhp (60.2kW)/l; 130lbft (174 Nm) @ 4500rpm. ENGINE STRUCTURE twin belt-driven ohc; 16-valves, multicam with VVC; aluminium cam cover, cam carrier, cylinder head, block, bearing ladder, sump, damp cylinder liners; MEMS electronic ign, multi-point fuel injection; 5-bearing crankshaft. TRANSMISSION rwd; sdp clutch; 5-speed manual synchromesh; final drive 4.2:1. CHASSIS steel monocoque structure; independent suspension by double wishbones, interconnected Hydragas springs, anti-roll bars; servo ventilated front disc brakes, 9.5in (24.1cm), solid at rear; ABS; rack and pinion, electric PAS; 11gal (50l) fuel tank; 5-spoke alloy wheels; 185/55 VR15 tyres front, 205/50 VR15 rear; 6J rims. DIMENSIONS wheelbase 93.7in (238cm); track 55.1in (140cm) front, 55.5in (141cm) rear; turning circle 34.45ft (10.5m); ground clearance 47.2in (120cm); length 154.1in (391.4cm); width 64.1in (162.8cm); height with hood 49.6in (126cm). PERFORMANCE max speed 130mph (209kph); 20.7mph (33.3kph) @ 1000rpm; 0-60mph (96kph) 7.0sec; 7.4kg/bhp (9.9kg/kW); fuel consumption 26.4mpg (10.7l/100km). PRICE £18,875.

1997 EX253 and 1998 EX255 Andy Green Utah car

In September 1997, Californian Land Rover technician Terry Kilbourne took MG back into the record books at Bonneville driving EX253, a specially prepared MGF, at 217mph (348.35kph) on the salt flats.

The car kept most of its standard features with the addition of a 40cm tapered tail, a flat-deck tonneau cover, a tear-drop canopy with a roll hoop and a lightning flash echoing the Gardner MG. The 1.8litre K-series engine was exchanged for a turbocharged 1.4litre producing 329bhp, 333PS (245.3kW) on super unleaded fuel.

Above: Andy Green with MG EX255 and EX181.

The following year's EX255 was a more formidable proposition. With a supercharged MG V8 in place of the customary MGF 4-cylinder, its aim was to beat the 254.9mph (409.2kph) set by Phil Hill in EX181 in 1959. Supercharging failed to deliver the required power, so it was turbocharged instead by Janspeed and driven in a record attempt by Andy Green, the Royal Air Force pilot who had broken the sound barrier in Thrust SSC.

Recognisably an MGF with wheel spats, tail fins, smooth undertray and a bubble canopy over the driving seat EX255 was resplendent in light metallic green. Failure of a clutch withdrawal bearing led to abandonment of the attempt during the 50th Bonneville Speed Week.

EX255: BODY lhd single-seat record breaker; weight 3086.4lb (1400kg). ENGINE 8 cylinders, 90 deg V; mid; 94mm x 86.4mm, 4797cc; 942bhp (702.458kW) @ 8000rpm; 196.4bhp (146.4kW)/l; 590lbft (800Nm) @ 16psi supercharger boost. ENGINE STRUCTURE pushrod ohv; hydraulic tappets; reinforced, cross bolted version of production aluminium cyl block; cyl heads engineered with large valves and improved porting; Omega forged pistons; valves inlet 1.9in diameter, exhaust 1.6in; forged H-section steel connecting rods; cam-driven mechanical centrifugal compressors feeding two water cooled heat exchangers; charge air temperatures not exceeding 30°C; exhaust 4 into one large bore manifolds and open twin exhausts; sequential fuel injection with self-learning strategy; no radiator, recirculating large capacity tank with heat exchanger; dry sump with twin scavenge pumps; 5-bearing crank machined from solid steel billet with 2.1in big end journals and 2.25in main bearings. TRANSMISSION rwd; 5.5" triple plate sintered AP racing clutch; modified Hewland type NMT 6-speed sequential transaxle installed upside down with a step up gear between engine and gearbox; GKN race specification drive shafts, Lobro inboard and CV outboard joints. CHASSIS Font body structure to rear bulkhead standard MGF steel construction; space frame in 2in seamless steel tubing rear of bulkhead to house new power unit; standard MGF steel panels for wings, bonnet and doors; demountable body panels in carbon fibre epoxy attached with Dzus fasteners; ifs, MGF double wishbone based with increased castor angle; Hyragas units non-interconnected with adjustable stiffened spring rates; lowered and restricted suspension travel as MGF Cup spec; front subframe retained solidly mounted using MGF Cup suspension mounts; irs, MGF double wishbone based; MGF Hyragas units non-interconnected with adjustable stiffened spring rates; MGF Cup Eibach dampers; geometry and travel modified to improve anti-squat, clearance to underbody profile. Rear space frame standard MGF. Hubs and bearings, front standard MGF; rear Range Rover. Brakes un-servoed 4 wheel ventilated cast iron discs as MGF Cup spec, discs increased from 260mm to 310mm; uprated competition callipers with high temp pads to 800°C; Mooneyes steel wheels; front 4.5Jx16, rear 7Jx18; Mickey Thompson tyres rated to 375+mph front 24.5 x 7.5 x 16; rear 26.5 x 9 x 18. Underfloor modifications for aerodynamics: 3-stage step diffuser; fuel tank 6.6gal (30l). Chrome Moly safety/roll cage; two carbon fibre AFFF 4000R fire extinguisher systems; 6 point seat belts; twin braking parachute system stored in 8in (20.3cm) dia tubes, 12ft dia high speed, 15ft dia low speed. Aerodynamics: Cd 0.180-0.195 dependent on aero aids used. Frontal area 1.48 sqm. Cda 0.266-0.289sqm. DIMENSIONS wheelbase 263cm (103.5in); track 140cm (55.1in) front, 125cm (49.2in) rear; length 456cm (179.5in (24.1cm)). Body extended by 400mm at rear with twin F18-style fins either side of bootlid extension. Width 163cm (64.2in); height 117cm (46.1in). PERFORMANCE maximum speed 255mph (409.351kph); 3.27kg/bhp (4.39kg/kW). PRODUCTION 1.

MG Project EX253. On 20 August, 40 years after Stirling Moss took EX181 to a 1500cc class speed record of 245.64mph (395.41kph), MG returned to the salt flats at Bonneville, USA, with a largely standard MGF (except for a longer tail and windscreen removed) to record 217.400mph (349.87kph), the fastest MGF ever.

1998 MGF Super Sports Concept

Geneva Motor Show surprises included a sequential gearchange and a supercharger for the MGF; and a showing of the K3 Magnette, chassis K 3001, raced in the 1933 Mille Miglia by Lord Howe. The MGF Concept looked like a regular MGF, with a composite plastic cockpit cover, racing tyres on aluminium wheels, aerodynamic guide vane strips on the lower sills and a huge air intake for the mid-engine reminiscent of the marine ventilators sported by MGs in the 1920s. Turbocharging was rejected on the grounds that the supercharger kept the engine within manageable rev limits, making it more suitable for the sequential automatic gearshift, a variation on the continuously variable transmission (CVT) steel belt transmission first seen on the Rover 200. Flared side panels on the aluminium body accommodated a wider track with large, rather dramatic wheels and low-profile tyres. Bumpers were carbon-fibre composites.

The show car had deep red bodywork and full length white tonneau, with chrome embellishments in the style of a modern racing MG. The cockpit had a raked low drag racing windscreen and the seats, fully trimmed in white leather with red stitching, reflected the white and chrome interior theme.

BODY roadster, 2 doors, 2 seats; weight approx 2337lb (1060kg). ENGINE 4 cylinders; mid transverse; 80mm x 89mm, 1796cc; compr 10.5:1; 197.3bhp (147.1kW); 109.9bhp (81.9kW)/l. ENGINE STRUCTURE twin belt–driven ohc; 16–valves; aluminium cam cover, cam carrier, cylinder head, block, bearing ladder, sump, damp cylinder liners; MEMS electronic ignition, multi–point fuel injection; supercharger and intercooler; 5–bearing crankshaft. TRANSMISSION rear wheel drive; sdp clutch; 5–speed manual synchromesh gearbox; final drive 3.938:1. CHASSIS steel and aluminium bonded structure; independent suspension by double wishbones, interconnected Hydragas springs, anti–roll bars uprated to racing specification; servo ventilated 29.5cm (11.6in) AP Racing disc brakes; ABS; rack and pinion, electric PAS; 11gal (50l) fuel tank; eight–spoke alloy road wheels; 210/605 R16 race tyres front; 220/640 R17 race tyres rear. DIMENSIONS wheelbase 93.7in (237.5cm); track 56.7in (143.9cm) front, 58.6in (148.9cm) rear; turning circle 34.45ft (10.5m); length 154.1in (391.4cm); width 64.1in (162.8cm). PERFORMANCE maximum speed approx 140mph (225kph); 0–60mph (96kph) 6.1sec; 5.4kg/bhp (7.2kg/kW). PRODUCTION 1.

A realistic representation of a modern weekend racer, its supercharger could also be regarded as a complete–combustion solution to California's clean–air legislation, particularly with the VVC engine.

2000 MGF

Above: The MGF range; 1.8i, 1.8i Steptronic and 1.8i VVC.

The MGF was not altered much for 2000, although a makeover of the interior brought new materials, including some convincing lookalike timber. Curiously, trompe d'oeil walnut or ash for the facia had not been disdained on some classic MGs when walnut veneer-on-plywood dashboard of the 1950s T-series gave way to Rexine, workmanlike for open cars. The plastic wood of the MGF was regarded much the same; not fake, merely sensible.

Instrument faces changed from cream to silver and there were new tyre and wheel options. However, the option of a Steptronic gearbox was more radical. There had been fully automatic MGBs and MGCs. The 1930s K3 and R-type had the novel Wilson preselector, ZB Magnettes of the 1950s briefly had the lacklustre semi-automatic Manumatic, but the MGF's Belgian-made ZF VT1 Ecotronic with wet clutch was something new. Its origins lay in the 1960s Daf belt-drive transmission but, with steel-segment pusher belts instead of rubber and fabric puller ones, its evolution was significant. Most importantly, the engine did not whine up to high rpm and wait until the transmission caught up with it. Steptronic could be regarded as a slick manual shift, with a flick of the lever or, if the driver chose, a reliable automatic that did not soak up power. MG authority Roger Parker said of CVT: "You see a noticeable loss of acceleration, especially from standstill, a 5.5% loss of fuel efficiency and it emits 6% more CO_2 than the same engine when attached to a manual gearbox".

VVC spec: BODY roadster, 2 doors, 2 seats; weight 2359lb (1070kg). ENGINE 4 cylinders; mid, transverse; 80mm x 89mm, 1796cc; compr 10.5:1; 145bhp (108kW) @ 7000rpm; 80.7bhp (60.1kW)/l; 128lb ft (174 Nm) @ 3000rpm.ENGINE STRUCTURE twin belt-driven ohc; 16-valves, multicam with VVC; aluminium cam cover, cam carrier, cylinder head, block, bearing ladder, sump, damp cylinder liners; MEMS electronic ign, multi-point fuel injection; 5-bearing crankshaft. TRANSMISSION rear wheel drive; sdp clutch; 5-speed manual synchromesh gearbox; optional Steptronic; final drive 4.2:1. CHASSIS steel monocoque structure; ifs by double wishbones, interconnected Hydragas springs, anti-roll bars; servo ventilated front disc brakes, 9.5in (24.1cm), solid at rear; ABS; rack and pinion, electric PAS; 11gal (50l) fuel tank; 5-spoke alloy wheels; 185/55 VR15 tyres front, 205/50 VR15 rear; 6J rims. DIMENSIONS wheelbase 93.7in (238cm); track 55.1in (140cm) front, 55.5in (141cm) rear; turning circle 34.45ft (10.5m); grnd clearnce 304.8in (20.3cm) (120cm); length 154.1in (391.4cm); width 64.1in (162.8cm); height with hood 49.6in (126cm). PERFORMANCE maximum speed 130mph (209kph); 20.7mph (33.3kph) @ 1000rpm; 0-60mph (96kph) 7.0sec; 7.4kg/bhp (9.9kg/kW); fuel consumption 26.4mpg (10.7l/100km). PRICE £20,819 Steptronic £19,990

2000 MGF Super Sports Mk II

The Super Sports concept of 1998 had been a bold initiative, although it did not have the unqualified blessing of MG's new owner, BMW. Conceived in what came to be known as the Gaydon skunk works operating, as Rob Oldaker famously described it, "under the Munich radar," the Super Sports concept was unveiled somewhat peremptorily at Geneva by the usually self-composed Bernd Pischetsreider. Press and MG devotees applauded and, although it did not have the crucial backing of the BMW management for production in 1999, in the end it gained a second wind.

A great deal had been learned from racing (in the MG tradition since the 1920s), particularly the MGF Cup series. In 1999 when the Super Sports appeared at Geneva it was essentially a road car with windscreen and road realistic equipment. Designer David Woodhouse had left to join General Motors, so his successors eradicated some of his racier features, leaving it with Recaro seats and Grenadine leather like the 75th anniversary MGF. The air intake was enlarged, the sequential gearbox dropped and same-size tyres used front and back. All that was wrong was the timing of its announcement. Rover was exhausted following the launch of the important 75 saloon and, by the time attention could be diverted to MG, so much had altered politically that it never had any real chance of going into production.

BODY roadster, 2 doors, 2 seats; weight approx 2337lb (1060kg). ENGINE 4 cylinders; mid, transverse; 80mm x 89mm, 1796cc; compr 10.5:1; 197.3bhp (147.1kW); 109.9bhp (81.9kW)/l. ENGINE STRUCTURE twin belt-driven ohc; 16-valves; aluminium cam cover, cam carrier, cylinder head, block, bearing ladder, sump, damp cylinder liners; MEMS electronic ign, multi-point fuel injection; supercharger and intercooler; 5-bearing crank.

TRANSMISSION rear wheel drive; sdp clutch; 5-speed manual; final drive 3.938:1. CHASSIS DETAILS steel and aluminium bonded structure; ifs by double wishbones, interconnected Hydragas springs, anti-roll bars uprated to racing specification; servo ventilated 29.5cm (11.6in) AP Racing disc brakes; ABS; rack and pinion, electric PAS; 11gal (50l) fuel tank; seam-welded 17in KN alloy wheels; 225/45-17 Goodyear Eagle F1 tyres.

DIMENSIONS wheelbase 93.7in (238cm); track 56.7in (143.9cm) front, 58.62in (148.9cm) rear; turning circle 34.45ft (10.5m); grnd clearance 304.8in (20.3cm) (120cm); length 154.1in (391.4cm); width 64.1in (162.8cm).

PERFORMANCE maximum approx 140mph (225kph); 0-60mph (96kph) 6.1sec; 5.4kg/bhp (7.2kg/kW).

2001 MGF Trophy; MGF 1.6i 112PS

The ink was scarcely dry on the agreement devolving control of Rover away from BMW, before MG Rover was formally created and more new MGFs introduced. Left to itself, the new management immediately extended the model's market coverage at both ends. At the top, as a further acknowledgment to MG's racing heritage, the MGF Trophy 160 Special Edition was equipped with a tuned version of the K-series 1.8litre VVC engine. This had a wide-bore exhaust, developed 10 per cent more power and promised new levels of performance still well within the MGF's well-balanced ride and handling. Competition spring and damper rates were applied to the interconnected Hydragas suspension, which also had a 2cm lower ride height; brakes were AP racing units with red MG-branded callipers. Lightweight forged and spun alloy wheels were an option and the aerodynamic qualities were enhanced by spoilers front and rear. At the lower end of the price scale the 1.6i had a shorter-stroke version of the K-series engine, losing scarcely any of the 1.8's vigour yet keeping the features that were making it popular. Electric power steering, driver's airbag, rake-adjustable steering wheel, anti-theft alarm, electric windows and alloy wheels were all retained at an effective price reduction of £1,500 on the 1.8i.

[1.6 in brackets] BODY roadster; 2 doors, 2 seats; weight 2370lb (1075kg). ENGINE 4 cylinders; mid, transverse; 80mm x 89.3mm [80mm x 79mm]; 1796cc [1589cc]; cr 10.5:1; 159bhp (118kW, 160PS) @ 7000rpm [111bhp (82kW, 112PS) @ 6250rpm]; 88.5bhp (65.7kW)/l [69.9bhp (51.6kW)/l; 128 lb ft (174 Nm) @ 4500rpm [107lbft (145Nm) @ 4700rpm]. ENGINE STRUCTURE Trophy belt-driven multi-cam 4 inlet, 1 exhaust, Variable Valve Control (VVC); 4 valves per cyl; aluminium cyl head and block; MEMS 3 engine management; 5-bearing crankshaft; [belt driven twin overhead camshaft, 4 valves per cylinder]. TRANSMISSION rwd; sdp clutch; 5-spd synchromesh manual gearbox; final drive 4.200:1 [3.938:1]. CHASSIS steel monocoque; ifs by double wishbones, interconnected Hydragas springs, telescopic dampers, anti-roll bars; servo ventilated front disc brakes 11.9in (30.4cm) [9.5in (24.1cm)], solid at rear; ABS, dual circuit; rack and pinion, electric PAS; 11gal (50l) tank; 195/45 R16 tyres 7J rims front, 215/40 R16 7Jrims rear, [185/55 front & 205/50VR15 tyres 6.0J rims rear]; multi-spoke alloy wheels. DIMENSIONS wheelbase 93.7in (238cm); track 55.5in (141cm) front,140cm (55.1in) rear; turning circle 34.65ft (10.6m); ground clearance 4.72in (12cm); length 153.9in (391cm); width 64.2in (163cm); height 49.2in (125cm) [49.9in (127cm)] with hood. PERFORMANCE max 137mph (220.5kph) [116mph (187kph)]; 20.7mph (33.3kph) @ 1000rpm [22.1mph (35.5kph)]; 0-60mph (96kph) less than 7.0sec [9.6sec]; 6.8kg/bhp (9.1kg/kW) [9.7kg/bhp (13.1kg/kW)]; fuel consumption 36.3mpg (7.8l/100km), Euro III emission standard, declared CO2 190g/km [38.4mpg (7.4l/100km), declared CO2 177g/km]. PRICE Trophy 160 £20,815; 1.6i £15,335.

The MGF Trophy 160SE was something of a fashion statement, with Trophy Yellow and Trophy Blue specially created for it, augmenting the popular Solar Red and Anthracite Black. Bright mesh grilles, body-colour inserts in the door casings and leather and fabric seats were among the features designed to secure its appeal.

2001 MG X20 X30

Almost as soon as the new MG Rover regime took control, its development policy for replacing the model range was revealed as threadbare. Strapped for cash despite the generosity of BMW's settlement for looking after the workforce, there was no improvement to speak of and it was a case of dressing up Rovers as MGs and hoping for the best.

The Rover 25 was not an unworthy basis for a sporty small saloon in the tradition of the Y-type with a bit more power and speed. Launched in 1995 as the Rover 200 this new edition came out in January 2001, X20 *(pictured in blue)* with a 2.5 V6 and 4 or 5 doors, X30 1.8VVC and 3 doors *(facia pictured below)*.

The K-series engine was now perhaps less likely to fall victim to the head gasket failures it suffered in the MGF. Better cooling and in-service modifications helped. Some restatement of the MG identity was necessary for the X series, achieved by cosmetic speed cues, aerodynamic aids, wings and spoilers, low-profile tyres and chunky aluminium wheels. Decorative chrome was reduced to a minimum and body colour was used for the MG grille and air intakes.

Designer Peter Stevens stripped out the wood-and-leather that had made Rovers seem perilously older-generation, replacing it with practical modern new-age textures like that of faux carbon-fibre or shiny metallics in the hope of securing appeal to younger buyers. Supportive upholstery was deemed necessary to give drivers what Rob Oldaker was fond of calling "outrageous fun".

The KV6 from the Rover 800 was a development of the K4 but had an indifferent reputation compared with the Honda 2.7 V6 it replaced.

Spec 1.6 4 cylinder [1.8 in brackets] BODY hatchback, saloon; 5 doors, 4 doors, 5 seats; weight 2447lb (1110kg), [2546.3lb (1155kg)]. ENGINE 4 cylinders; front transverse; 80mm x 79mm [80mm x 89.3mm], 1589cc [1796cc]; compr 10.5:1; 108bhp (80kW, 109PS) @ 6000rpm [116bhp (86.5kW, 117PS] @ 5500rpm; 68bhp (50.3kW)/l [64.6bhp (48.2kW)/l]; 102lbft (138Nm) @ 4500rpm [118lbft (160Nm) @ 2750rpm]. ENGINE STRUCTURE 2 belt-driven overhead camshafts; 4 valves per cylinder; aluminium block and head; MEMS3 engine management; 5-bearing crankshaft. TRANSMISSION front wheel drive; sdp clutch; 5-speed manual synchromesh gearbox; final drive 3.765:1 [3.938:1]. CHASSIS steel monocoque structure; ifs by double wishbone and coil springs; irs multi-link with coil springs; telescopic dampers and anti roll bars front and rear; disc front, drum rear dual circuit brakes; ABS; rack and pinion PAS; 12.1gal (55l) fuel tank; 205/50 R16 tyres, 6.5J rims. DIMENSIONS wheelbase 103.1in (262 cm); track 58.3in (148cm) front, 57.9in (147cm) rear; turning circle 33.9ft (10.36m); ground clearance 5.3in (13.5cm) saloon; length h/b 171.7in (436cm), saloon 180in (452cm); width 66.9in (170cm); height 53.9in (137cm). PERFORMANCE maximum speed 118.3mph (189.9kph) [121.5mph (195kph)]; 19.9mph (32kph) [35kph (21.801mph)] approx @ 1000rpm; 0–60mph (96kph) 10.3sec [9.3sec]; 10.3kg/bhp (13.9kg/kW) [9.6kg/bhp (12.8kg/kW)]; fuel consumption 39mpg (7.23l/100km) [30.7mpg (9.2l/100km)].

2001 MGF 1.8i 120PS; sequential CVT, 1.8VVC MG TF

Over the years MG sports cars had often had ambitions to be racing cars. Some were. When superchargers were in, MGs had them. When all-enveloping bodywork arrived, MGs had that too, although it with parsimonious and sometimes fractious management it took a little time to evolve from TF to MGA.

In modern times once engines moved firmly behind drivers, in due course they belatedly moved behind in MGs too. MG drivers were entitled to enjoy the virtues of a low polar moment of inertia, so when racers got round to changing gear with buttons on the steering wheel it seemed only natural for MG drivers to follow suit. The Constant Velocity Transmission (CVT) of the Belgian ZF Getriebe NV Sint-Truiden was an integrated engine and transmission unit that introduced electronic steps in the continuous (stepless) performance of the CVT. The reception accorded the 1999 introduction of sequential gear shifting was less than enthusiastic however, *Autocar* offering only the faintest praise after finding too many decisions were taken out of drivers' hands. There was, furthermore, loss of performance over a similar car tested in 1995. Fuel consumption suffered with testers blaming the frequency with which the sequential car's engine revved up to the 6,000rpm limit. It increased from an average of 26.4mpg (10.7l/100km) and a best of 33.6mpg (8.4l/100km) to 22.7mpg (12.4l/100km) and 32.6mpg (8.7l/100km). This effectively reduced the range from contents of the 50 litre tank to under 300miles (482.8km). MGF range *(pictured)* with Starlight Silver and red hood on TF160, now with heated glass rear screen and Ignition Blue TF 135 with 'V-Spoke' alloy wheels.

[VVC in brackets] BODY roadster; 2-doors, 2-seats; weight 2370lb (1075kg). ENGINE 4-cyl; mid, transverse; 80mm x 89.3mm, 1796cc; compr 10.5:1; 119bhp (88kW, 120PS) @ 5500rpm [143bhp (107kW, 145PS]; 66.3bhp (50kW)/l [79.6bhp (59.6kW)/l]; 121lbft (165Nm) @ 3000rpm [128lbft (174Nm) @ 4500rpm]. ENGINE STRUCTURE twin belt-driven overhead camshafts; [multi overhead cams four inlet, one exhaust] 4 valves per cyl; aluminium cyl head, block; MEMS3 engine management; 5-bearing crankshaft.

TRANSMISSION rwd; sdp clutch; 5-speed manual synchromesh gearbox; final drive 3.938:1. Optional ZF CFT23 Electronic 6-speed sequential, final drive 4.05:1. CHASSIS steel monocoque; ifs by double wishbones, interconnected Hydragas springs, telescopic dampers, anti-roll bars; servo ventilated front disc brakes 30.4cm (11.9in), 9.5in (24.1cm), solid at rear; ABS, dual circuit; rack and pinion, electric PAS; 11gal (50l) fuel tank; VR18 tyres 7J rims, multi-spoke alloy wheels. DIMENSIONS wheelbase 93.7in (238cm); track 55.5in (141cm) front, 55.1in (140cm) rear; turning circle 34.6ft (10.6m); ground clearance 4.7in (12cm); length 153.9in (391cm); width 64.2in (163cm); height 1.6i 50in (127cm) with hood. PERFORMANCE maximum speed (manufacturer's figure) 120mph (198kph) [130mph (209kph)]; 26.1mph (42.1kph) manual, 22.3mph (35.9kph) sequential @ 1000rpm in top (6th speed position) manual selection; 0-60mph (96kph) 10.4sec [7.0sec]; 9kg/bhp (12.2kg/kW) [7.5kg/bhp (10kg/kW); fuel consumption combined 38.4mpg (7.4l/100km [36.3mpg (7.8l/100km)]. PRICE: 1.8 £16,851; VVC £19,315; Trophy £20,815

Longbridge MG TF Assembly line (Pre production phase), May 2007.
Image code. MG_ANJ_001

Under the new ownership MGF production was reinstated briefly at Longbridge in 2007.

2001 MG X10

The Rover 75, designed under BMW, was a masterpiece. BMW engineering was accomplished and looked it. The outside of the engine was exquisitely finished, so it stood to reason that the inside must be exemplary as well. Close-grained castings with no rough edges were technical accomplishments.

Yet BMW looked flustered when it took over Rover in 1994, even though the logic was impeccable. Buyers often avoided BMWs for their assertiveness. They wanted cars that were understated with a smooth ride, silky engine, longevity and even gadgetry, while disliking BMW's image. They wanted something discreet; a Rover built to BMW standards of integrity seemed tempting to all parties. Accordingly, the Rover 75 was commendable even though there was a whiff of German whimsy in the oval instruments and clubby interior. It seemed a bit like what a German thought a British car should be. Still, it was beautifully proportioned, lively rather than fast and the epitome of good taste.

The traditional grille and carpeted luxury exemplified all that had been best about "One of Britain's Fine Cars". It was, alas, less successful as an MG. It should have had the appeal of a ZA or ZB Magnette but BMW had deliberately and carefully made it unlike a BMW. With appliqué MG badges and cosmetics it seemed merely contrived. The X10 was a pastiche, neither refined nor racy. It was made as saloon and an estate car designated unimaginatively X11. Its clientele was ill-defined and it did little to stem the brand's fall from grace.

BODY 5-door hatchback, 4-door saloon; weight 2712lb (1230kg), 2789lb (1265kg). ENGINE 6 cylinders, 90deg V; front; 80mm x 82.8, 2497cc; compr 10.5:1; 175bhp (130kW, 177PS) @ 6500rpm; 70.1bhp (52.1kW)/l; 177lbft 240Nm @ 4000rpm. ENGINE STRUCTURE 4 belt-driven overhead camshafts; 4 valves per cylinder; turbocharger and intercooler; aluminium cylinder head, aluminium block; DFI engine management; 4-bearing crankshaft. TRANSMISSION front wheel drive; sdp clutch; 5-speed manual synchromesh gearbox; final drive 3.89. CHASSIS steel monocoque structure; ifs by double wishbone and coil springs; irs multi-link with coil springs; telescopic dampers and anti roll bars front and rear; disc front, drum rear dual circuit brakes; ABS; rack and pinion PAS; 12.1gal (55l) fuel tank; 205/50 R16 tyres, 6.5J rims [205/45 R17, 7J rims]. DIMENSIONS wheelbase 103.1in (262 cm); track 58.3in (148cm) front, 57.9in (147cm) rear; turning circle 33.9ft (10.36m); ground clearance 5.3in (13.5cm) saloon; length h/back 171.7in (436cm), saloon 178in (20.3cm) (452cm); width 66.9in (170cm); height 53.9in (137cm). PERFORMANCE max speed 115.2mph (185kph); 25.8mph (41.4kph) @ 1000rpm; 0-60mph (96kph) 10.6sec; 7kg/bhp (9.5kg/kW) fuel consumption 50.5mpg (5.6l/100km).

2001 MG–Lola EX257 Le Mans prototype

Pictured with (left to right) Mark Blundell, Julian Bailey, Kevin McGarrity, Johnny Kane and (inset) Anthony Reid and Warren Hughes.

MG's last hurrah at Le Mans was with MG-Lola EX257, which took part in 2001-2003. Lola had form at Le Mans. In 2000 three Lola B2Ks were entered, one with a Judd, another with a Ford engine as Le Mans Prototype (LMP) 900s. The Automobile Club de l'Ouest (ACO) had changed the regulations to admit two different classes of prototype, and LMP675 was for smaller turbocharged engines in lighter more manageable cars to compete with the bigger, more powerful LMP900s. A third Lola in the 2000 race, designated a B2K/40 with a Nissan engine, finished 29th and won the LMP625 category. The Judd and Ford cars in the senior class showed promise but failed to finish.

The Lolas' performance provided MG with an opportunity to try and get back to the big league. It was struggling to re-make its sporting name in touring cars and by the new millennium there was no real requirement for racing cars to be actually built in the factories whose name was on the front. Mercedes-Benzes made in Milton Keynes were soon to come in Formula 1 and a class win at Le Mans would look good. Lola built MG B01/60 to LMP675 regulations taking a number of design elements from the successful B2K/40 acquiring a traditional MG Experimental number EX257. The front apron was nearly identical to its predecessor, so it looked more convincing for the nose to be recognisably different. A square airbox that looked vaguely like an MG grille and sidepods with long sweeping lines to manage airflow along with a turbo intake on top offset like the production MGF Super Sports did the trick. The rear wing was low down to reduce drag and EX257 was light, around 690kg (1521.2lb) against the minimum 675kg (1488.1lb).

The Nissan engine had to be replaced. Advanced Engine Research (AER) used MG's own 2.0litre turbocharged XP20 as the basis for a Garrett turbocharged 4-cylinder known as the MG XP20. It gave 500bhp (373kW) limited by regulation air restrictors, and two EX257s were entered for Le Mans 2002 by MG Sport & Racing Ltd set up for the occasion. They qualified 14th and 17th overall and were fastest LMP675 competitors. During the test days earlier in the year team manager Hugh Chamberlain, worried that the cars looked small and unspectacular and could be somehow sidelined for the race proper, making representations to the notably quirky ACO to make certain they became starters.

In the event problems showed early on. The modified production engines were highly stressed and although the ACO had introduced rules to widen the scope of the entry, it looked as though endurance racing would be too much for small power units. By 9.30 one MG driven by Reid, Hughes and Kane retired after losing oil pressure, although the second of Blundell, McGarrity and Bailey ran 12 hours before its engine gave up.

Still, the XP20 engine had done well, so for 2003 the MG team returned with two EX257s. The Blundell, McGarrity and Bailey car qualified a commendable 6th. Reid, Hughes, Kane 12th, both running among the expected-to-win LMP900 Audis. Their reliability was improved as well, one surviving until 2am and the other until 8am. One was put out by gearbox problems, the other by engine failure. A third car entered by American Knight Hawk team unfortunately caught fire during the night.

Two years of being unable to finish at Le Mans and financial strain on MG Rover led to cancellation of the project, a solitary entry from Intersport failing to finish in 2004 following engine failure after 102 laps. Lola continued selling the cars to customers along with Advanced Engine Research. Dyson Racing replaced Knight Hawk Racing in the American Le Mans Series, EX257 winning every race to give Dyson the championship. James Weaver and Butch Leitzinger won the Infineon Raceway round, the first time for an LMP675 car. For the final Petit Le Mans Intersport replaced the turbocharged MG engine with a naturally aspirated Judd KV675 V8, the resulting mechanical changes making it a B01/60, and providing effectively an LMP675 win.

2002 MG ZR 1.4, 1.8

By the spring of 2001, the X designation was amended to Z as efforts continued to make the most of the MG brand. ZR was related to the Rover 25, ZS to the 45. Kevin Howe, Rob Oldaker and Peter Stevens were contriving a generation of MGs in what they regarded as the Kimber tradition of enhancing a series-production car.

The ZS was effectively the ZR with an additional 4.7in (12cm) on the wheelbase, most of the extra 19.7in (50cm) accounted for by the saloon's 470litre boot. The 5-door was 6.3in (16cm) shorter, offering 720litres of luggage space with the seats flat. The good proportions of both cars were unimpaired and to try for a racy feel spring-stiffening continued front and rear. Forty per cent stiffer springs and a 2cm lower ride height not only gave it roll stiffness and body control that seemed appropriate to an MG that seemed in tune with its target audience. The steering rack ratio changed from 18.1:1 to 16.4:1 to give faster response.

Kimber's legacy of Safety Fast, it was claimed, held good. *Autocar* was not impressed: "You can say what you like about mutton dressed as lamb, but you can't argue with the value of MG's facelifted hot hatch. Determined haggling will slash the ZR's £14,995 list price to around £12,625, and there's not much else around like it for that sort of money. Remember the MG's value, and you can forgive some of its foibles. This is indisputably an old car, pepped up by recent revisions to exterior styling (largely successful), cabin (less so) and minor mechanical changes (mixed). Its age is apparent from the moment you grasp the old 1990s' flexi-key, an unfortunate reminder of the ZR's ancient roots."

[1.8 in brackets] BODY hatchback, saloon; 5 doors, 4 doors, 5 seats; weight 2447lb (1110kg), [2546.3lb (1155kg)]. ENGINE 4 cylinders; front transverse; 80mm x 79mm [80mm x 89.3mm], 1589cc [1796cc]; compr 10.5:1; 108bhp (80kW, 109PS) @ 6000rpm [116bhp (86.5kW, 117PS) @ 5500rpm; 68bhp (50.3kW)/l [64.6bhp (48.2kW)/l]; 102lbft (138Nm) @ 4500rpm [118lbft (160Nm) @ 2750rpm]. ENGINE STRUCTURE 2 belt-driven overhead camshafts; 4 valves per cylinder; aluminium block and head; MEMS3 engine management; 5-bearing crankshaft. TRANSMISSION front wheel drive; sdp clutch; 5-speed manual synchromesh gearbox; final drive 3.765:1 [3.938:1]. CHASSIS steel monocoque structure; ifs by double wishbone and coil springs; irs multi-link with coil springs; telescopic dampers and anti roll bars front and rear; disc front, drum rear dual circuit brakes; ABS; rack and pinion PAS; 12.1gal (55l) fuel tank; 205/50 R16 tyres, 6.5J rims. DIMENSIONS wheelbase 103.1in (262 cm); track 58.3in (148cm) front, 57.9in (147cm) rear; turning circle 33.9ft (10.36m); ground clearance 5.3in (13.5cm) saloon; length h/b 171.7in (436cm), saloon 180in (452cm); width 66.9in (170cm); height 53.9in (137cm). PERFORMANCE maximum speed 118.3mph (189.9kph) [121.5mph (195kph)]; 19.9mph (32kph) [35kph (21.801mph)] approx @ 1000rpm; 0-60mph (96kph) 10.3sec [9.3sec]; 10.3kg/bhp (13.9kg/kW) [9.6kg/bhp (12.8kg/kW)]; fuel consumption 39mpg (7.23l/100km) [30.7mpg (9.2l/100km)].PRICE 1.4 £9,850; 1.8 160 £14,860.

2002 MG ZS 1.8 117ch, 2.5 V6 177ch, 2.0 diesel

MG Rover bypassed the 2.0litre KV6 for the 2.5litre, in what it regarded as the foundation ZS to form the basis of MG's official re-entry into the British TOCA Tour race series. MG had been out of saloon car racing since tentative forays with the Y-type 1¼litre cars of the 1950s. The ZS with the full-house racing version of the 175bhp (130kW) 6-cylinder was looking for outright countrywide wins rather than worthy but ultimately less satisfactory class victories in the clubby confines of Silverstone, Oulton Park or Snetterton.

The performance of the lusty 4-cylinder diesel would have seen it among the leaders in 1951, when Dick Jacobs and Ted Lund were struggling round the old Silverstone circuit in 2min 18sec at about 75mph (120.4kph). Stirling Moss's 3.4 Jaguar was just breaking 2min at 86.7mph (139.2kph). The 2002 road ZS enjoyed modern chassis engineering with 17in wheels, firmer suspension, improved brakes, and steering designed for keen drivers. Wind-tunnel testing was used to confirm the aerodynamic package of skirts and spoilers designed to minimise drag and lift. Sports exhaust tailpipes were housed within a heat shield to fit into the rear bumper and provide satisfactory ground clearance. The interior also came in for the MG generic treatment, with specially contoured sports seats holding occupants in place on fast corners.

[2.5 KV6 in brackets] BODY 5-door hatchback, 4-door saloon; weight 2712lb (1230kg), 2789lb (1265kg). ENGINE 4 [6] cylinders, in-line [90deg V]; front transverse; 84.5mm x 89mm [80mm x 82.8], 1994cc [2497cc]; compr 19.5:1 [10.5:1]; 99bhp (74kW, 100PS) @ 4200rpm [175bhp (130kW, 177PS) @ 6500rpm]; 49.6bhp (37.1kW)/l [70.1bhp (52.1kW)/l]; 177lbft (240Nm) @ 2000rpm [177lbft 240Nm @ 4000rpm]. ENGINE STRUCTURE belt-driven single overhead camshaft [4 belt-driven overhead camshafts]; 2 [4] valves per cylinder; turbocharger and intercooler; aluminium cylinder head, cast iron [aluminium] block; DFI engine management; 5-bearing [4-bearing] crankshaft. TRANSMISSION front wheel drive; sdp clutch; 5-speed manual synchromesh gearbox; final drive 3.938:1 [3.89]. CHASSIS steel monocoque structure; ifs by double wishbone and coil springs; irs multi-link with coil springs; telescopic dampers and anti roll bars front and rear; disc front, drum rear dual circuit brakes; ABS; rack and pinion PAS; 12.1gal (55l) fuel tank; 205/50 R16 tyres, 6.5J rims [205/45 R17, 7J rims]. DIMENSIONS wheelbase 103.1in (262 cm); track 58.3in (148cm) front, 57.9in (147cm) rear; turning circle 33.9ft (10.36m); ground clearance 5.3in (13.5cm) saloon; length h/back 171.7in (436cm), saloon 178in (20.3cm) (452cm); width 66.9in (170cm); height 53.9in (137cm). PERFORMANCE maximum speed 115.2mph (185kph); 25.8mph (41.4kph) @ 1000rpm; 0-60mph (96kph) 10.6sec; 12.4kg/bhp (16.6kg/kW) [7kg/bhp (9.5kg/kW)] fuel consumption 50.5mpg (5.6l/100km). PRICE 1.8 120 £13,130; 2.5 180 £16,215.

2002 MG ZT 2.5 V6 190, 180, 160ch

ZT 260 V8 SE pictured with monogram aurora paintwork

There was a choice in premium-range MG versions of the Rover 75. Customers were offered two front-drive cars with different versions of the KV6 and, right at the summit of the new order, a rear-drive car with a powerful V8.

The engineering of the 75 was almost beyond reproach. It had been evolved with the utmost care by BMW and was made to the highest standards. It had been more than half a century since the comparatively hit and miss nature of MG engineering at Oxford and to a lesser degree Abingdon prevailed. That had not been unsuccessful, producing some commendable cars, but it depended heavily on the skill, talent and experience of a handful of people; Albert Sydney (Syd) Enever (1906-1993), Hubert Noel Charles (1893-1982 and effectively chief engineer of MGs since the 1930s), Gerald Palmer (1911-1999), Reg Jackson, and Cec Cousins had all produced great commercially successful designs.

However by the 1990s international safety, environmental and sometimes seemingly fatuous regulations made such demands that a laissez-faire approach was no longer appropriate. Huge teams of designers and engineers now had to be deployed on new cars so almost all were satisfactory and quite a lot exemplary. When it came to the ZT, even though its basis was in many ways ready-made, there were neither the personnel nor the resources to carry it through.

[190PS in brackets] BODY saloon; 4 doors, 5 seats; weight 3186lb (1445kg). ENGINE 6 cyl, 90deg V; front transverse; 80mm x 82.8mm, 2497cc; compr 10.5:1; 159bhp (118.6kW, 160PS) @ 6500rpm [198bhp (147.7kW, 190PS) @ 6500rpm]; 63.7bhp (47.5kW)/l [79.3bhp (59.2kW)/l]; 177lbft (240Nm) @ 4000rpm. ENGINE STRUCTURE 4 belt-driven overhead camshafts; 4 valves per cyl; aluminium cyl head and block; Siemens engine management; 4-bearing crankshaft. TRANSMISSION front wheel drive; sdp clutch; 5-speed manual synchromesh gearbox; final drive 3.944:1. CHASSIS steel monocoque structure; ifs by MacPherson strut with coil springs; irs Z-axle with coil springs; anti roll bars front and rear; telescopic gas-filled dampers; front disc, rear drum dual circuit brakes; ABS; rack and pinion PAS; 14.25gal (64.8l) fuel tank; 225/45 R18 tyres, 7.5J rims. DIMENSIONS wheelbase 108.1in (274.6cm); track 59.25in (150.5cm); turning circle 37.3ft (11.4m); ground clearance 6.1in (15.5cm); length 186.9in (474.7cm); width 70in (178cm); height 55.3in (140.4cm).
PRICE: 2.5 160 £18,415; ZT-T 2.5 estate £21,265.

2003 MG ZT XPower V8

At a press conference revealing the V8 ZT 120 (pictured) at Longbridge early in 2001, it was suggested that work on it had been under way for some time although perhaps still well behind schedule. Press events in the declining years of MG Rover seemed staged as much to reassure the firm's financial backers as they were to lure customers. Product Development Director Rob Oldaker vouchsafed no details beyond the bare essentials and a car displayed may not have had an engine. The bonnet was firmly locked. All Oldaker would claim was that the exceptional torsional stiffness of the Rover 75 body shell enabled development of a rear wheel drive edition capable of dealing with 256.4bhp (191.2kW 260PS) from a substantial Ford V8 known as "modular" because machinery in plants where it was made at Romeo, Michigan and Windsor, Ontario could be reconfigured to make different versions. The only common feature was its 100mm cylinder bore spacing enabling manufacture on the same transfer machines.

While there were few practical limits to the power that could be transmitted through front wheel drive (electronics could by now almost eliminate torque steer and wheelspin) MG Rover took the view apparently that an all-weather road car needed rear wheel drive or better still four wheel drive. By any prognosis production was probably a year or more away, but when the car did make its appearance it would be a fine flagship for a new range with promises of a number of sub-species. Out went the Rover's whimsical oval instruments and wood veneer. In, according to Oldaker, would come an aircraft-style facia appropriate for a 21st century sports saloon.

BODY saloon; 4 doors, 5 seats. ENGINE 8 cylinders, 90deg V; front; 90.2mm x 90mm; 4600cc; comp 9.4:1; 256.1bhp (191kW) @5250rpm; 41.5bhp (30.9kW)/l; 302lbft (409Nm) @4000rpm. TRANSMISSION rwd; Hydratrak automatic, final drive 3.73:1. CHASSIS steel monocoque structure; ifs by MacPherson strut with coil springs; irs with coil springs; anti roll bars front and rear; telescopic gas-filled dampers; disc dual circuit brakes; ABS; rack and pinion PAS; 14.2gal (64.6l) fuel tank; 225/45 R18 tyres, 7.5J rims. DIMENSIONS wheelbase 108.1in (274.6cm); track 59.25in (150.5cm); turning circle 37.3ft (11.4m); ground clearance 6.1in (15.5cm); length 186.9in (474.7cm); width 70in (178cm); height 55.3in (140.4cm).

2003 MG X80 Qvale Mangusta

The MG X80, shown in Birmingham in September 2001, never attained production in any numbers. One exhibited at the Glasgow Motor Show with an ill-fitting plastic windscreen gave the game away. By now in terminal decline, MG Rover looked increasingly desperate, introducing cars as unrealistic as they were expensive, to brace the confidence of lenders, shareholders, suppliers, or an increasingly sceptical government. The X80 was a cobbled-up coupe of dubious quality. The partly carbon fibre body was made in Italy in the old De Tomaso factory, and the engine was another Ford V8 of 4601cc producing upwards of 320bhp (238.8kW) @ 6000rpm according to specification. At upwards of £65,000 it looked a poor bargain.

Kjell Qvale was a Norwegian-American entrepreneur importing European cars, including MG and Austin-Healey, to the West Coast. He was involved in the disappointing Jensen-Healey of the 1970s and, as Qvale Automotive, he homologated the Qvale Mangusta, made in Italy for the US market. It was based on an unremarkable 1996 concept of the troubled De Tomaso Company, the Bigua, which had failed to get into production. The ambitious Qvale took it on, launched it in 2000 and hoped to set up production in Modena.

MG Rover saw an opportunity to shortcut three years' of development and official homologation, took over Qvale Automotive Srl in Italy, allocated the project code X80 setting up a subsidiary company, MG X80 Ltd, to produce it.

The proposition was that a new model based on the Qvale Mangusta would sell in America, which was once again buying extravagant cars and importantly was the one place where broadly

speaking the design was already legal. The numbers were not big but at premium prices it could be profitable, or so it was put to MG Rover bankers and sponsors.

The MG X80 had been a conservatively styled concept in 2001 but a so-called production model, renamed MG XPower SV *(right),* was provided with a more aggressive appearance by designer Peter Stevens and launched the following year. Clay model to production car was reputedly done in 300 days by a Swedish company to achieve a price of under £100,000. The entry level car cost £65,000, the uprated XPower SV-R £83,000. Projected top speed was 165mph (265.5kph) and 0-60 in 5.3sec. There was airy talk of a track car with a 5.0litre engine and nitrous-oxide injection of 1000bhp (745.7kW), which would have its speed governed to 195mph (313.8kph).

A complicated production process used carbon fibre body panels made in the UK by SP Systems and then shipped to Belco Avia near Turin for assembly into bodywork. These were in turn made into a complete body shell on a box frame chassis and running gear and taken back to MG Rover at Longbridge to be trimmed and finished. Some exterior and interior parts were borrowed from Fiats, the headlights from a Punto and rear lights from a Fiat Coupe. The modest aim of 130 cars a year was hopelessly optimistic. The MG XPower SV Club claimed 82 cars were produced excluding four pre-production prototypes, but probably only a dozen ever actually found paying customers. Some pre-production and show cars were dismantled before production was stopped due to lack of sales. A few final ones were sold to customers in 2008.

Museum Piece. 2004 SV-R languishes in the British Motor Museum, which has the world's largest collection of historic British cars. Opened in 1990, it has over 300 of them from collections of the British Motor Industry Heritage Trust and the Jaguar Heritage Trust including most significant MGs. Banbury Road, Gaydon, Warwick CV35 0BJ.

Timeline of MG from 1965

1965

Jul: BMC makes offer for Pressed Steel effective September 1965.

Jul 22: Rover buys Alvis.

Oct 20: MGB GT at Earls Court.

1966

Jun: Leonard Lord, now Lord Lambury, retires from BMC board. George Harriman becomes chairman, Joe Edwards managing director.

Jul 11: BMC and Jaguar agree merger, finalised in December.

Oct 19: MG Midget Mark III (GAN4) launched at Earls Court with 1275cc A-series engine. Also Austin-Healey Sprite Mark IV.

Nov 3: Assembly of pre-production MGC begins at Abingdon, two months after Healeys reject BMC's proposed Austin-Healey 3000 Mark IV. 13 pre-production MGCs built for development.

Dec 11: Leyland agrees merger with Rover, effective March 1967.

Dec 14: BMC and Jaguar announce joint company: British Motor Holdings. Joe Edwards becomes BMH chief executive under Sir George Harriman.

1967

Feb: Industry Minister Anthony Wedgwood Benn announces exploratory talks between Leyland and BMH in House of Commons.

Mar: BMC Competitions Manager Stuart Turner replaced by Peter Browning.

Oct 18: MGC, MGC GT and MGB Mark II at Earls Court. MG 1100 Mark II launched.

Oct: Merger discussions between BMH and Leyland follow meeting at Chequers between George Harriman (BMH), and Donald Stokes (Leyland), at the invitation of prime minister Harold Wilson

Nov 6: Design centre established at Cowley under Roy Haynes. Dick Burzi keeps small studio at Longbridge.

Nov: first cars to meet new US safety and emissions requirements built with 'Abingdon Pillow' padded dashboards and dual-circuit brakes. Austin-Healey 3000 Mark III discontinued. Single car built for UK in May 1968.

1968

Jan: Harris Mann joins Austin-Morris styling studio.

Jan 17: £320m merger of Leyland Motor Corporation with BMH forms British Leyland Motor Corporation. Cars divided into Austin-Morris (including MG) and Specialist Cars (with separate Rover, Triumph and Jaguar boards).

Apr: MG 1300 replaces 1100 Mark II. Joe Edwards resigns from BMH prior to formation of BLMC. Harry Webster and George Turnbull, ex Triumph, in charge of Austin-Morris.

MG 1300 furnishings (above) were up-market.

Apr 8: Production of Magnette Mark IV ends.
May 14: Creation of British Leyland Motor Corporation.
May 22: Roy Haynes proposes MG ADO28 (Morris Marina).
Aug: Harry Webster announces advanced engineering and conservative styling policy for Austin, more style and conservative engineering for Morris.
Aug 5: BLMC board views three ADO28 prototypes by Pininfarina, Michelotti, and Roy Haynes. Haynes's proposals accepted.
Sep: Sir George Harriman retires.
Oct 15: Earls Court Motor Show. Sir Donald Stokes instructs competitions department to go only for outright wins.
Oct 16: MG 1300 Mark II inaugurated at motor show; 2-door only

1969
Apr: Austin-Morris design transferred from Cowley to studio formerly occupied by Dick Burzi. Interior design remains at Cowley until October.
Jun 27: John Thornley retires, Les Lambourne now assistant general manager.
Jul: Riley 1300 production discontinued; Riley 4/72 carries on until October.
Aug 4: MGC production ceases.
Sep 18: Last MGC leaves Abingdon.

Sep 19: BLMC board approves ADO67, the Austin Allegro of 1973.

Oct 11: British Leyland facelift MG Midget and MGB recessed matt black grilles.

Oct 15: Mini Clubman and 1275GT at Earls Court. Austin and Morris 1300 GT effectively replaces MG 1300. Austin-Morris interior design Cowley to Longbridge.

Nov 5: Abingdon starts work on mid engined ADO21.

1970

Jan: Roy Haynes leaves BLMC.

Autumn: Engineers Spen King & Mike Carver visit USA to research market for new TR sports car. Competition between Austin-Morris styling Longbridge, Triumph Canley and Michelotti. MG Abingdon not invited to put forward mid-engined ADO21.

The 1970 MG ADO70 consigned to Gaydon was among efforts to create a sports car based on the Issigonis Mini. Keen drivers so enjoyed the handling of the small front wheel drive saloon, it almost looked as though it would supplant the traditional sports car at which MG had been adept for 40 years. Initiatives were also being tried in case it became necessary to replace the MG Midget when it looked as though America might outlaw open cars altogether. It seemed prudent to have a sporty small saloon ready just in case. The project was only abandoned over worries about other safety and emissions regulations in the USA. Known as the Michelotti Mini although styled by Paul Hughes at Longbridge, this prototype was built by Michelotti but although based on a 1275GT Mini turned out heavy and never came close to production. Special feature: 'Targa' detachable roof panels to provide an open-car feel.

Oct 14: Austin Maxi 1750 introduced at Earls Court, with longer-stroke E4 engine planned for ADO 21.

Oct 31: Abingdon Competitions Department closes. Special Tuning a low-cost unit.

Nov 4: MG ADO21 full-size clay viewed by British Leyland management.

Dec 29: Work ceases on ADO21.

1971

Jan: Austin-Healey Sprite rebadged Austin. Healey royalties cease.

May 27: 250,000th MGB, left-hand-drive Blaze MGB GT, made at Abingdon.

May: Enever retires as chief engineer. Roy Brockleburst takes over.

Jul: Austin-Morris styling studio MG Magna proposal for new BLMC corporate sports car approved, and becomes Triumph TR7. Last Mini Cooper, last Austin Sprite.

Aug 4: Abingdon instructed to build MGB GT V8, following assessment of Costello car.

Aug 31: MG 1300 Mark II discontinued.

1972

Mar: Rover-Triumph created under Sir George Farmer. Board has seven Rover and five Triumph members.

Spring: MG SSV1 experimental safety vehicle shown at Washington road safety exhibition.

May 4: MG Midget with round rear wheel arches.

Aug: MGB range facelifted for 1973 MY.

Sep: O-series engine emerges as overhead-cam B-series. Soft bumpers approved for MGB.

Nov 6: Last MGB produced in Australia.

Dec 12: Production of MGB GT V8 starts.

1973

Feb: British Leyland plans MGB in case TR7 is late; O-series engine is due by April 1974

Jul: Roy Brocklehurst transferred to BL Advanced Engineering.

Don Hayter becomes chief engineer at Abingdon.

Aug 15: MGB GT V8 launched.

Sep: Bumper overriders for MG Midget, MGB and MGB GTs in the USA.

1974

Jan: Work starts on ADO88.

Summer: O-series engine decision for MGB and Marina by 1977 model year, autumn 1976. Delayed to 1978 MY.

Jul: British Leyland cash crisis. Banks talk of £150m loan.

Oct 16: Soft bumpers for Midget, MGB, MGB GT and MGB GT V8. Midget adopts Triumph Spitfire 1493cc engine.

Nov 27: Banks and government discuss BLMC's finances.

Dec 3: Triumph Spitfire 1500 launched in UK with same engine as Midget 1500.

Dec 6: Tony Benn tells Parliament government guarantees BLMC's capital.

Dec 18: Sir Don Ryder, governmental industrial advisor, appointed to investigate BLMC by March.

1975

Jan 1: MGB GT withdrawn from USA.

Jan: Triumph TR7 two-door sports coupe announced for sale only in USA.

26 Mar: Ryder Report recommends government contribution of £2.8 billion over seven years; company split into four divisions: cars, trucks and buses, international, and "special products".

May: David Bache appointed design director.

Jun: Overdrive made standard on UK-market MGBs.

Jun 27: British Leyland Motor Corporation renamed British Leyland; government 99.8% shareholder.

Aug 11: British Leyland formally nationalised.

Sep: Endurance testing of prototype O-series engines in MGB, Princess and Morris Marina.

Sep 13: First post-Ryder marque realignment. Austin-Morris 18-22 series renamed Princess.

Dec 16: Government secures Chrysler UK with £162.5m.

1976

May 19: Triumph TR7 introduced in UK and Europe.

Jun: MGB withdrawn from Continental Europe.

Rover SDI 3500 launched with aluminium 3528cc V8.

Jul: Last two MGB GT V8s finished at Abingdon - production ended in June.

1977

Jan: Work restarts on "federalizing" O-series engine for MGB, aiming for introduction in 1980.

Feb: pilot-build of Triumph TR7 Sprint and TR7 V8 begins at Speke.

Nov 1: Michael Edwardes joins British Leyland.

1978

Jan: ADO88 replaced by larger LC8 project.

Feb: Edwardes reveals plan to reorganise Austin-Morris including MG, and Jaguar-Rover-Triumph.

Feb 15: Proposal for Speke factory to close and move TR7 production to Canley.

Apr 1: BL Motorsport Abingdon homologates TR7 V8 rally car.

Apr 3: government provides £450m equity in British Leyland.

May 26: Triumph TR7 production ends at Speke. TR7 Sprint and Lynx cancelled.

TR7 V8 – the TR8 – delayed two years.

Jul 1: British Leyland renamed BL. Leyland name remains on commercial vehicles. Austin-Morris is under Ray Horrocks, and Jaguar-Rover-Triumph under William Pratt-Thompson.
Development MGB with O-series engine presented to BL management.
Approval of £275m for LC8 Metro.
Jul: 1.7- and 2litre O-series engines introduced in Princess 2 range.
Aug 8: John Z DeLorean builds factory in Belfast Northern Ireland for making sports cars with government grants.
Aug: BL in exploratory talks with Honda.
Sep: 1.7-L O-series engine for Marina 2. MG becomes part of Jaguar-Rover-Triumph.
Oct: Triumph TR7 production restarts at Canley after five-month gap. US dealers unhappy with deliveries.

1979
Apr 1: Peter Mitchell joins BL Heritage, later British Motor Heritage.
Apr: US-market MGB Limited Edition (LE) model introduced at New York Motor Show.
May 15: Memorandum of understanding between BL and Honda. New Triumph saloon to be built at Canley based on Honda Ballade/Civic. Introduction planned for October 1981.
Jun: Sharp rise in strength of sterling affects BL, in particular US exports. BL forms CORE (Co-ordination of Resources) strategy. Edwardes Plan streamlines company.
Jul 9: BL meets industry minister Sir Keith Joseph to discuss funding of LC10.
Jul: Triumph TR7 convertible launched five years after TR7 coupe, for USA only.
Aug: Midget production runs down; among the last are 500 for Japan.
Assembly of Vanden Plas 1500 transferred to Abingdon.
Golden Jubilee celebrations at Abingdon.
Sep 10: Announcement of closure at AEC Park Royal. BL plans to end production of MG sports cars at Abingdon and manufacturing at Canley.
Sep 13: John Thornley invites 445 US Jaguar-Rover-Triumph-MG dealers to urge BL to continue MGB production.
Sep 26: BL claims loss of £900 on every MGB. Austin Allegro 3 launched.
Sep 30: MG clubs stage London protest rally
Oct 14: Alan Curtis of Aston Martin Lagonda and Peter Sprague in the USA prepare bid for MG marque and MGB.
Oct 16: Curtis discusses bid with consortium.
Oct 17: Union leaders recommend BL workers accept Edwardes Plan.
Oct 18: Consortium led by Aston Martin Lagonda announces bid to take over MG name and factory.
Nov 1: BL workforce ballot: 80% vote, of which 87.2% accepts Edwardes Plan

Nov 6: Californian MG dealers and 416-strong US JRT dealer council threaten to sue BL for £100m if MGB is withdrawn. BL says MGBs will remain available until 1981, pledges to keep the MG marque.

Dec 12: Last MG Midget down Abingdon production line. Black UK-specification car for British Motor Heritage brings total to 224,817.

Dec: BL discusses MG Boxer project, low-cost MG offshoot from Triumph TR7, to placate US JRT dealers. Idea abandoned early in 1980, and MG returned to Austin-Morris from JRT.

Dec 20: BL says government agrees to recovery plan and a further £205m.

1980

Jan: 500,000th MGB, a black roadster, built at Abingdon.

Jan 14: Jaguar-Rover-Triumph press release: "MGBs will be produced until late 1980 … available into early 1981. The MG name will be retained and there are plans to build a successor to the MGB when production ends at Abingdon."

Mar 31: Aston Martin consortium meets BL board, proposing £30m deal for exclusive world-wide licence to MG name and Abingdon factory.

Apr: Triumph TR7 production begins at Rover in Solihull, overlapping with production at Canley.

Jul 1: Aston Martin announces nearly half required £30m has been withdrawn. Last hope is that Japanese and Arab backers provide £12m. Aston Martin makes a quarter of its workforce redundant.

Jul 2: William Pratt-Thompson, head of BL International, announces Abingdon factory to be sold.

Jul 4: Alan Curtis talks with Japanese in an effort to acquire funds for take-over.

Jul 9: BL car divisions reorganised again: JRT dissolved, Jaguar becomes separate once more. Volume cars (Austin-Morris) absorbs Rover and Triumph to form Light Medium Cars (LMC). Cars Commercial looks after marketing and product planning. Triumph Spitfire discontinued. LM10 approved by BL board for 1983 launch.

Aug: last production-specification MGB bodyshell produced at Pressed Steel, Stratton St Margaret, Swindon.

Oct 8: Austin Metro launched.

Oct 17: Austin Metro at NEC Motor Show, Birmingham.

Oct 23: last MGB goes down the line at Abingdon.

Oct 24: MG factory at Abingdon closes.

1981

Jan: £990m further state funding of BL over next two years.

Jan 26: announcement by BL of last MGB derivative, the UK-only MGB and MGB GT LE.

Feb: Henry Ford II acquires one of the last US-specification MGB LEs for the Ford Museum.

Mar 18-24: Auction of MG factory contents: 434 buyers, 3600 lots, totalling £100,000 for BL.

May 10: BL claims Jaguar loses £2m per month due to unfavourable dollar/sterling exchange.

May 13: Ray Horrocks of BL announces closure of Solihull Rover factory for all but Land Rover.

May 16: final auction of Abingdon contents.

Jun 15: BL Motorsport moves to Cowley. Plans laid for MG Metro 6R4.

Jul 26: *Sunday Times* says BL plans MG-badged version of the Metro.

Aug 6: MG is among names considered for performance Metro.

Sep: Austin Allegro discontinued.

Oct 7: Triumph Acclaim launched.

Nov 12: Ray Horrocks and Honda sign co-operative agreement in Tokyo for new executive car, coded XX.

1982

Jan: Banks agree to lend BL £277m over 8-10 years. David Bache resigns as design director following management disagreements. Replaced by Roy Axe, formerly of Chrysler.

May: Austin Rover Group formed from Austin, Morris, MG, Rover and Triumph. Harold Musgrove chairman and chief executive.

May 5: MG Metro 1300 announced.

Jul 1: BL announces Morris name to be phased out.

Oct 22: MG Metro Turbo announced at motor show.

Nov: Sir Michael Edwardes leaves BL, publishes *Back From The Brink*.

1983

Feb: MG Metro 6R4 prototype handed over by Williams Engineering to Austin Rover Motorsport at Cowley.

Mar 1: Austin Maestro range includes MG1600.

Apr: new director of interior design is Richard Hamblin, reporting to Roy Axe. Gordon Sked is director of exterior design.

Jun 11: Interim facelift for Metro includes MG.

1984

Mar 31: MG Metro 6R4 competition debut; a Yorkshire rally with Tony Pond.

Apr 25: Montego range includes 2litre fuel-injected MG version with O-series engine. S-series replaces R-series in MG Maestro 1600. LC10 has cost £210m. BL reports first operating profit, £4.1m, since 1978.

Jun 19: British Motor Industry Heritage Trust (BMIHT) appoints David Bishop, formerly materials control manager at Austin-Morris Body Plant Cowley, assistant MD.

Aug 10: Jaguar privatised. Government keeps "golden share" until end of 1990.

Sep: Austin Rover formed as LMC is integrated with Cars Commercial.

Oct 3: MG Maestro 2.0 EFi replaces 1.6litre S-series-engined version.

1985
Apr 3: MG Montego Turbo.

May 8: Harold Musgrove announces Austin Rover Cars of North America (ARCONA) in partnership with Norman Braman to launch Austin Rover/Honda XX in the USA in 1987.

Jun: FISA bans four-wheel drive Group B cars for 1987, substituting Group S and limiting power to 300bhp (223.7kW).

Sep 19: MG EX-E concept car launched at Frankfurt Motor Show.

Nov 1: MG Metro 6R4 homologated for international debut on RAC Rally.

1986
Feb 2: Roy Hattersley tells Parliament General Motors wants to buy Leyland Trucks and Land Rover.

Apr: MG Maestro introduced in Japan. Design studios at Canley reorganised: Gordon Sked director of production design studio; Richard Hamblin director of concept design studio.

May 1: Graham Day appointed chairman of BL.

May 2: Henri Toivonen and Sergio Cresto killed in Lancia Delta S4 Group B rally car.

May 3: Jean-Marie Balestre of FISA announces Group B rally cars banned from January 1987; Group S abandoned.

Jul: BL renamed Rover Group

Jul 15: Honda/Rover joint project XX launched as Rover 800 series.

Sep: Harold Musgrove leaves Rover Group.

Dec: David Bishop starts British Motor Heritage MGB bodyshell project.

1987
Apr 18: US-market Sterling (Rover 800) launched at New York Motor Show.

May: Austin Rover Motorsport Division at Cowley closed down.

Nov: Sterling 800 range on sale in the USA.

1988
Feb 29: First MGB bodyshell produced at Faringdon.

Mar 1: British Aerospace (BAe) talks with government on acquisition of Rover.

Mar 30: British Aerospace buys Rover Group for £150m; government writing off £800m debt. £2.98 billion in state aid received since 1975.

Apr 13: British Motor Heritage launches MGB bodyshell.

Oct 22: MG Maestro Turbo, to be built by Tickford, announced at Birmingham Motor Show.

Dec 19: MG-badged coupe, based on planned cabriolet derivative of the Rover 200 (R8), photographed for the archives.

1989

Jan: Rover board restructured. Graham Day hands over to George Simpson (Baron Simpson of Dunkeld, left), board members reduced from 36 to 11. John Towers becomes production engineering director and Graham Morris takes over as Sterling president from Chris Woodwark.

Jul 14: Honda announces £300m first European assembly plant at Swindon, and 20% equity stake in Rover. Rover takes 20% stake in HUM (Honda UK Manufacturing).

Sep 18: Graham Day suggests sports car. Appoints Project Phoenix to investigate three MG concepts with different engine/drive train configurations: PR1, PR2 and PR3. 'PR' stands for Phoenix Route, nicknamed 'Pocket Rocket'.

Oct 11: New Rover 200 range launched at London Motorfair. First production application of K-series engine.

Oct: Roy Axe takes charge of Rover's advanced design studio. Richard Hamblin works on Project Phoenix, and places contracts for running prototypes.

Dec 1: Shareholders accept Ford's cash offer for Jaguar.

1990

Mar 28: Executive committee approves activities leading to Rover Special Products (RSP) running prototypes.

Mar: Work starts on Heritage MGB V8 project; Mark Gamble builds prototype at Snitterfield, to be completed by May.

May 2: Launch of revamped Metro with 1.1- and 1.4litre K-series engines. Top of range GTi not an MG.

Jun: Rover board reviews PR1, PR2, PR3 and PR4 (similar to PR2, but with a steel body). PR3 increased in size.

Sep 19: Graham Day tells press, "We are going to do a proper MG."

1991

Jan: Rover commissions consultants MGA and ADC to develop styling clays based on mid-engined PR3. John Towers becomes MD in charge of product supply.

Apr: Rover Special Products researches significance of MG badge to potential customers.

May: Two styling models for PR3 presented. Rover approves PR3 from development to D Zero.

Jun: Customer clinic tests of sports car concepts; leads to rejection of pop-up headlamps and abandonment of PR5, seen as a Jaguar/Aston Martin style, not MG. Rover management approves RV8.

Jul: proposal of PR3 1.6litre K-series engine with optional supercharger.

Aug 9: Rover Group drops US Sterling marque; servicing back-up for Sterling models maintained.

Sep: Gerry McGovern begins work on styling clay for PR3 at Canley.

Autumn: MG-badged saloons discontinued after MG Maestro and Montego 2.0i.

Dec: Roy Axe forms independent consultancy. Gordon Sked now in charge of Rover design.

1992

Jan: MG RV8 prototype presented at Rover dealer conference.

Jan 22: Styling of PR3 clay model approved.

Mar 3: Geneva show. Rover 200 Cabriolet launched (Project Tracer nearly became an MG). Rover 800 coupe also launched.

Mar: Styling of PR3 approved. Rover staff invited to give opinions on "elements of an MG".

Jun: Teaser brochure for RV8 issued with studio photograph of DEV1 prototype, "The Shape of Things to Come".

Sep 18: MG Car Club, MG Owners' Club and others invited to preview of MG RV8 at Canley.

Oct 20: RV8 launched by John Towers at Birmingham Motor Show, together with Rover 200 coupe.

Nov: Rover board approves 1.8litre K-series with optional VVC.

Dec: PR3 design signed off. Mayflower and Rover agree Mayflower Vehicle Systems (the merged Motor Panels and IAD) to raise £24m for design, engineering and production of bodyshells.

1993

Mar: Rover board approves PR3. Launch planned for 1995.

Mar 31: Mayflower investment includes rights issue to raise £34.6m. Production of over 10,000 a year expected, with sales of £20m for a 6-year contract.

Mar 31: First production MG RV8 made at Cowley for BMH museum (chassis Nr 251, British Racing Green metallic). First six customer cars completed on 19 Apr.

Apr: Rover 620 launched.

Oct: Woodcote Green MG RV8 at Tokyo Motor Show.

1994

Jan 13: First 46 RV8s leave Southampton for Japan.

Jan 31: British Aerospace sale of Rover Group to BMW AG for £800m.

Feb 21: Honda relinquishes 20% shareholding in Rover, which releases its 20% in Honda's UK manufacturing subsidiary.

Mar 18: Title and ownership of Rover Group officially transferred to BMW AG. Rover Group comprises two sub-groups: Rover Group Holdings plc, Birmingham (with 89 subsidiaries) and Rover Group USA Inc, Lanham, Maryland (with four subsidiaries).

Jul: Pre-production examples of MGF completed, using final tooling.

Sep: Pilot production of MGF.

1995

Feb 6: Preview of MGF for MG Car Club, MG Owners' Club, Octagon Car Club at Gaydon.

Feb 20-24: Dealer MGF launch.

Mar 7: MGF launched at Geneva.

May: Rover 416 and 420 launched.

Aug 4: First volume-production MGF built at Longbridge CAB2.

Sep 23: First customer MGF deliveries.

Oct: MGF makes its UK and Japanese Motor Show debuts.

Nov: Rover 214 and 216 launched.

Nov 22: Last MG RV8, Woodcote Green bound for Japan.

1996

Feb 1: MGF awarded Japanese Import Car of The Year. 300 MGFs sold in Japan, and a further 1200 ordered.

Feb 21: Test session at Castle Combe for Japanese journalists to drive MGF development car.

Jun 1: John Towers resigns from Rover BMW

Sep 1: Walter Hasselkus becomes chief executive of Rover Group.

Oct: Rover 200vi launched.

1997

Jul 4: Unions and Rover BMW management agree 3 year deal for jobs and investment.

1998

May 20: Rover Oxford plan inaugurated

Jul: Rover reduces workforce by 3000.

Aug: Unions and BMW agree changes in working practices.

Sep: Rover BRM Limited Edition 200

Oct 21: Rover 75 replaces 400 and 600; sales and productivity warning.

Dec: Hasselkus retires, replaced by Bernard Sämann.

On show at British Motor Musuem Gaydon 1998 MG EX255 record car. Plaque detail:

*'In 1959 the American Grand Prix driver Phil Hill set the record for the fastest MG
at 254.91mph reached on the Bonneville Salt Flats Utah, USA in MG 181. To coincide with the 50th Speed Week at
Bonneville in 1998, MG set a goal to break that record, which hadn't been beaten in nearly 40 years.'*

To challenge the record MG designed EX255, a streamliner based on the MGF shape, constructed from a steel tube subframe. The special bodywork, built by Mayflower of Coventry, uses standard MGF parts for the doors and front wings but other panels are made from carbon fibre. The engine, engineered by Janspeed and based on the faithful Rover V8, is mounted behind the driver, who changes gear using a 6-speed sequential system. EX255 rolls on special tyres, designed for very high speed and is stopped by uprated disc brakes and two parachutes.

Who was chosen to drive the fastest MG in the world? Naturally the fastest man on earth, Andy Green, who piloted Thrust SSC to a World Land Speed Record of 730.035mph. Under the small canopy, Andy sits in an alloy seat, designed specifically for him.

Initially EX255 was supercharged but this proved to be an Achilles' heel and the record attempt was abandoned until 1999. The car returned to Bonneville, this time with a more reliable twin-turbocharged engine but problems with the clutch meant the team ran out of time yet again.

EX255 has been stripped down in order to prepare it for another challenge to EX181's record. Following the sale of MG Sport and Racing during March 2006, the Trust was able to acquire

EX255. It is hoped to restore the car to its record breaking specification and display it with MG's other three streamliners, including EX181, as the last in a line of MG record cars. Top Speed 255mph (410kph).

1999
Feb 5: Bernd Pischetsreider and Wolfgang Reitzle resign from BMW board.
Aug: MGF designer Gerry McGovern leaves.
Oct: Rover 25 replaces 200 series. Rover 45 replaces 400 series.
Oct: BMW and Alchemy engage in talks about Rover's disposal.

2000
Mar 16: Alchemy Partners led by Jon Moulton makes unsuccessful bid for Rover.
May: Phoenix consortium buys Rover from BMW for £10. BMW retains Mini. Phoenix consists of former chief executive John Towers, Nick Stephenson and David Bowes (Lola Engineering), Terry Whitmore (Mayflower), John Edwards (Rover dealers), Brian Parker (non-executive) and Peter Beale. Parker and Whitmore later resign. Rover brand retained by BMW, licensed to MG Rover, sold to Ford, which bought Land Rover from BMW.
May: Kevin Howe appointed CEO Longbridge.
June: Chris Bowen operations director, Bob Beddow human resources, John Parkinson sales and marketing, John Millett finance and strategy, Rob Oldaker product development join management board.
Jul 7: Peter Stephens, former McLaren, Lamborghini, Jaguar, and Lotus designer joins MG Rover.
Aug: Plan announced for Le Mans joint venture with Lola.

2001
Jan 30: New MG range on show at Longbridge. Rover production line moved to Longbridge. Factory and rights to Mangusta bought from Qvale. Introduction of MGZR, ZS, ZT.

2002
MGTF introduced. Co-operation agreement with Tata Motors. Talks with Brilliance China Auto on building MGs and Rovers in China.

2003
MG X-Power SV and SV-R based on Qvale Mangusta. V8 variants of Rover 75 and MG ZT. Longbridge factory sold to St.Modwen Properties and leased back.

2004
MG ZR, ZS, ZT revised. Collaboration proposals talks with Shanghai Automotive Industry Corporation (SAIC). Design rights to Rovers sold to SAIC for £67m.

2005
Apr 8: Collapse of MG Rover. Ceases trading, debts of over £1.4billion. Price Waterhouse Cooper appointed administrators.
Apr 10: Government loan of £6.5m to cover week's wage bill.
Apr 15: SAIC negotiatons fail
Jul 22: Nanjing Automobile Group buys entire assets for £55m.

2006
Nanjing plans to make cars at Longbridge. Leases site for 33 years. SAIC introduces Roewe brand after failing to secure Rover name. Ford secures rights to Rover brand name, leaving only MG to be used on Nanjing cars.

2007
Nanjing produces MGTF in China.
Dec 26: SAIC and Nanjing join forces.

2008
Limited production of MGTF at Longbridge. Jaguar Land Rover sold to Tata Motors.

2009 MGTF 135 made at Longbridge. Department for Trade and Industry report reveals five executives took £42m in pay and pensions as MG Rover collapsed.

2010
MG6 produced at Longbridge from Chinese kits.

One of the largest-ever gatherings of some 5,000 MGs was at the Silverstone International
on 23-25 July 2004 (above), celebrating 80-plus years of MG.
Rob Gammage, chief executive of the MG Car Club (left) and Rob Oldaker MG Rover Product Development Director
with a selection of cars including "Old Number One" and the XPower SV.
There was an 80th Anniversary special edition of the MGF.

Chronology of MG Sports

1965
Austrian Gold Cup Rally: 1st.
Brands Hatch 1000 Miles Race: 1st, and 1st 2nd and 3rd in class.
Bridgehampton 500 Miles Race, USA: 4th, 1st in class.
GT Constructors' Championship: Midget 2nd in class; MGB 3rd in class.
Kingsway Trophy Race, Phoenix Park, Dublin: 1st 2nd 3rd 4th and 5th.
Le Mans 24-hour race: Hopkirk/Hedges (MGB 39) 11th of 14 finishers, 98.25mph (158.11kph), 2nd GT 2litre.
Sebring 12-hour race: Brennan/Morrell (MGB 49) 2nd in class, 10th prototype, 25th overall; Pricard/Pease (MGB 48) 6th in class, 10th GT, 32nd overall. Mac/Hedges (Midget 68) 1st in class, 12th GT, 26th overall.
Targa Florio: Hopkirk/Hedges (Midget GT 'Jacobs' coupe 44) 2nd in class, 11th overall.

1966
Austrian Alpine Rally: 2nd in class.
Brands Hatch 500 Miles Race: 3rd, two class wins.
Circuit of Ireland Trial: class win.
Circuit of Mugello Race, Italy: 3rd GT.
Class G Championship, USA: 1st.
Marathon de la Route 84-hour race at the Nürburgring: Vernaeve/Hedges ('Old Faithful' 47) outright winners after 5260 miles (8464.92km); Roger Enever/Alec Poole (MGB 46) retire.
Montlhéry 1000 Km Race: 2nd and 3rd in class.
Scottish National Speed Championship: 1st.
Sebring 12-hour race: Manton/Mac/Brown (MGB 59) 1st in class, 3rd GT, 17th overall.
Spa 1000 Km Race, Belgium: 1st GT, 1st in class.
Surfers Paradise 12 Hours Race, Queensland, Australia: class win.
Targa Florio race: Makinen/Rhodes ('Old Faithful' 64) 1st GT, 9th overall. Hedges/Handley (MGB 66) 2nd 2litre GT, 3rd in GT class.

1967
Amasco Racing Championship: 1st.
Berglandfahrt Rally, Austria: 1st.
London Rally: class win.
Monza 1000 Km Race: class win.
Rallye de Styrie Orientale, Austria: 1st.

Sebring 12-hour race: first MGB GT entry. Makinen/Rhodes in 'Old Faithful' (48) with 1824cc 8-series engine 3rd GT, 12th overall; Hopkirk/ Hedges (MGB GT 30) with 2004cc B-series engine 1st in class, 3rd prototype, 11th overall.

Spa Sports Car GP, Belgium: class win.

Targa Florio, Sicily: Hopkirk/ Makinen (lightweight MGB GT) 3rd in class, 9th overall.

1968

Sebring 12-hour race: Hopkirk/Hedges in 'Mabel' (MGC GTS 44) 1st in class, 3rd prototype, 10th overall; Rodriguez/McDaniel/Bill Brack (MGB GT 66) 5th in class, 18th overall; Truitt/Canfield (Midget actually Austin-Healey Sprite) 1st in class, 1st sports car, 15th overall; Waldron/Gammon/Scott (MGB 67) 7th in class, 31st overall.

Marathon de la Route: Fall/Fledges/Vernaeve (MGC GTS 4) 6th overall.

Targa Florio, Sicily: 2nd Sports.

84 Hours Marathon, Nürburgring, Germany: class win.

1969 Sebring 12-hour race: Hopkirk/Hedges (MGC GTS 35) 9th prototype, 15th overall; Hill/Brack (MGC GTS 36) 15th prototype, 34th overall; Truitt/Blackburn (MGB GT 62) 8th GT, 28th overall; Colgate/Parks (MGB 99) 5th in class, 32nd overall; Waldron/Scott/Donley (MGB 64) 6th in class, 38th overall

1970

Sebring 12-hour race: Belperche/Gammon/Mummery (MGB 57) 25th overall, Scott/Lanier/ Houser (MGB 58) next.

1971

Sebring 12-hour race. Neither MGB (51 and 52) finishes.

1978 Sebring 12-hour race. Kleinschmidt/Culpepper/Koch (MGB 52) 14th in class, 30th o/a.

1984 MG Metro 6R4 competition debut in a rally in Yorkshire, driven by Tony Pond.

1985 MG Metro 6R4 homologated for its international rally debut on the RAC Rally.

1987 Group B rally cars banned from January, and planned Group S abandoned.

2001-2003 MG relaunches a works motor sport campaign. EX257 entered for Le Mans 24 Hours Grand Prix d'Endurance. See text. MG ZS entered in the British Touring Car championship. MG ZR entered in the British Rally Championship.

2004

WSR races MG ZS. Plans to race Supertouring V8 MG ZT in the Deutsche Tourenwagen Masters (DTM) abandoned.

2006
WSR races MG ZR as Team RAC.

2007
MG ZR driven by Luke Pinder wins class N1 in British round of World Rally Championship.

Above: Claimed for a Guinness World Record as the world's fastest estate car the MG ZT-T Bonneville run by So-Cal Speed Shop of Pomona, California did 225.6mph (360.9kph) in the 2003 44th Bonneville Speed Week on the Utah Salt Flats. Driven by Pat Kinne, the event was recorded on video by MG executive Rod Ramsey.

Acknowledgments

We're pleased to make the MG File available as both a paperback and ebook downloadable on Kindle and electronic devices, with the continued help and support of Andrew Barron. Eric Dymock has added and amended that manuscript throughout, to create the MG Classics series in three parts.

For the MG File in 2001, acknowledgments were as follows and continue to be relevant. "The publishers thanked Kevin Howe, chief executive officer of MG Rover and his staff, in particular Gordon Poynter, Greg Allport, and Kevin Jones for their help in making the first edition of MG File possible. Nothing contributes to knowledge of any make so much as driving its cars, and for that the author thanked generations of public relations officials of MG, BMC, and their predecessors and successors for making available test cars of every MG since the 1950s. His thanks also went to MG owners who enabled him to take the wheel of cars made in the 30 years before 1950. Recognition also went, although not without reservations, to salesmen and restorers responsible for the author's ownership of MGs.

MG cars are so well documented that the publishers' quest for accuracy was challenging. We consulted widely to try and get things right and were grateful to all the MG clubs, in particular to Roche Bentley, Richard Monk, and Richard Ladds of the MG Owners' Club for their unstinting help and encouragement, especially their help in obtaining photographs. Robert Gammage and Peter Browning of the MG Car Club were equally heartening to the compilers of yet another MG book, adding to the wealth of material available. The late Roger Stanbury, who was not only an early MG owner and Vintage Register chairman, but also Dove Publishing's solicitor, was of great help and support. Roger provided critical comment at every stage of the book's production and invaluable contacts with MG authorities on whose experience the author drew, including Darrell Cocup with his files and memorabilia concerning John Thornley and Syd Enever. These included authors too Phil Jennings and Roger Barraclough whose Oxford to Abingdon was a definitive work, Mike Hawke whose K3 Dossier was invaluable, Malcolm Green, and Geoff Radford who generously made the Wilson McComb archives available. Among the MG historians whose work was invaluable were David Knowles the post-1945 equivalent of Jennings and Barraclough, Andrew Roberts, Simon Goldsworthy and Stewart Roy who kindly read the finished manuscript with the benefit of their long experience of MG. Among the photographic sources we used were the National Motor Museum at Beaulieu. As with all Dove Publishing books, our thanks were due to Andrew Barron for jacket design."

MG Bibliography

Combat, Barré Lyndon, William Heinemann London, 1933

Circuit Dust, Barré Lyndon, John Miles, 1934

Grand Prix, Barré Lyndon, John Miles 1935

Wheelspin, More Wheelspin, Wheelspin Abroad, CAN May

Racing Round the World, Count Giovani Lurani

Motor Racing and Record-Breaking, George Eyston and Barré Lyndon

Safety Last, George Eyston

Fastest on Earth, George Eyston

Magic MPH, Lt Col ATG Gardner, Motor Racing Publications, 1951

The Life of Lord Nuffield, PWS Andrews, E Brunner, Basil Blackwell Oxford, 1955

Maintaining the Breed, John Thornley, Motor Racing Publications London, 1950-1956

The MG Companion, Kenneth Ullyett, Stanley Paul, 1960

Out on a Wing, Sir Miles Thomas, Michael Joseph London, 1964.

The Bullnose and Flatnose Morris, L Jarman & R Barraclough, David & Charles 1965

MG Magnette K3, Wilson McComb, Profile Publications, Leatherhead, Surrey, 1966

MG 18/80, Wilson McComb, Profile Publications, 1966

MG M-type, Wilson McComb, Profile Publications, 1967

The Bullnose Morris Cowley, L Jarman RI Barraclough, Profile Publications 1967

The MG Story, JN Wherry, Chilton Books, 1967

The Magic of MG, Mike Allison, Dalton Watson 1972

MG The T Series, Richard Knudson (ed) Motorcars Unlimited, Savannah, Ga, USA, 1973

MG The Sports Car America Loved First, and MG: The Sports Car. Richard L Knudson Motorcars Unlimited Oneonta NY, 1975

The Bullnose and Flatnose Morris, Lytton Jarman & Robin Barraclough, 1976

An MG Experience, Dick Jacobs, Transport Bookman Publications London, 1976.

The MGA, MGB, and MGC, Graham Robson, Motor Racing Publications London, 1977

MG and Austin Healey Spridgets, Chris Harvey

The MG A, B, & C, Chris Harvey

The Immortal T Series, Chris Harvey, Oxford Illustrated Press, 1977

MG, Wilson McComb, Osprey London 1978 (Story of MG, Dent, 1972 revised)

British Leyland, The truth about the cars, Jeff Daniels, Osprey, 1980

The T-Series MGs, Graham Robson, Motor Racing Publications London, 1980.

The Sprites and Midgets, Eric Dymock, Motor Racing Publications London, 1981

MG Past and Present, AF Rivers Fletcher, Gentry Books, 1981

MGB, Wilson McComb, Osprey London, 1982

MGA, Wilson McComb, Osprey London, 1983

MG File, Martin Buckley (Ed), Classic and Sportscar Bay View Books, Bideford, 1987

The Cars of BMC, Graham Robson, Motor Racing Publications, 1987

The MG Log, Peter Haining (Ed), Souvenir Press London 1988.

The Kimber Centenary Book, Richard L Knudson (Ed) The New England MG T Register Oneonta NY, 1988.

The Magic of the Marque, Mike Allison, Dalton Watson London 1989, (pb 1972, revised)

Early MG, PL Jennings, PL Jennings, Llanbister, 1989.

MG Sports Cars, Autocar archive, various publishers incl Hamlyn, Bay View, 1980s.

Original MG T Series, Anders Ditlev Clausager, Bay View Books Bideford, 1989.

Original MGB, Anders Ditlev Clausager, Bay View Books

Original MGA, Anders Ditlev Clausager, Bay View Books

Original Sprite & Midget, Terry Horler, Bay View Books

Essential MG T-series Anders Ditlev Clausager, Bay View Books, 1989

MG Midget 1961-1979 and other Brooklands Books' compliations

MGB The Complete Story, Brian Laban, Crowood, 1990

MGB, Lindsay Porter, Haynes, 1992

MGB restoration and maintenance, Jim Tyler Osprey 1992

MG Midget and Austin-Healey Sprite restoration, Jim Tyler Osprey 1993

K3 Dossier, Mike Hawke, Magna Press, Leatherhead, 1992

MGB Illustrated History, Jonathan Wood, Lionel Burrell, G T Foulis, Haynes, 1993.

MG Gold Portfolio, Brooklands Books Ltd, Cobham, Surrey

Spriteley Years, John Sprinzel, Patrick Stephens, 1994

MG Road Cars Vol 1, 4 cylinder ohc 1929-1936, Malcolm Green, Magna 1994

The MG Collection, Richard Monk, Vol 1 pre-war models, Patrick Stephens 1994

The MG Collection, Richard Monk, Vol 2 post war models Patrick Stephens 1995

MG Trials cars, Roger F Thomas, Magna, 1995

Project Phoenix, The Birth of the MGF, Ian Adcock, Bloomsbury, 1996

MG Road Cars, Vol 2, 6 cylinder ohc 1931-1936, Malcolm Green, Magna 1997

MG Sports Cars, Malcolm Green, Bramley Books, 1997

Rallying in a works MG, Len Shaw, Magna, 1997

MG The Untold Story, David Knowles, Windrow & Green, 1997

MG Collectibles, Michael Ellman-Brown, Bay View Books, 1997

MG Britain's Favourite Sports Car, Malcolm Green, Haynes, 1998

Auto Architect, Gerald Palmer, Magna, 1998

MG from A to Z, Jonathan Wood, Motor Racing Publications, Croydon CR0 3RY 1998

Oxford to Abingdon, RL Barraclough and PL Jennings, Myrtle Pub., Cwmfrain, 1998

MGs on Patrol, Andrea Green, Magna, Leatherhead, 1999

The Works MGs, Mike Allison & Peter Browning, Haynes, 2000

MGF, David A Knowles, Haynes, 2000
MG Saloon Cars, Anders Ditlev Clausager
BMC Competitions Department Secrets. Marcus Chambers, Stuart Turner, Peter Browning, Veloce Publishing, 2015
Don Hayter's MGB Story, Veloce 2014

Among the sources used in research were the author's archive collections of the Swiss annual Automobil Revue/Revue Automobile published by Hallwag, Automobile Year published by Editions J-R Piccard, Autocourse published by Hazleton, and also of The Motor, The Autocar, Autosport, Motor Sport, Classic Car, Classic & Sportscar, The Automobile, Safety Fast and Enjoying MG, Automobile Quarterly, and Veteran & Vintage magazine to all of whose proprietors motoring historians owe continuing thanks.

The Author

Motherwell-born, trained as an engineer, Eric Dymock joined the road test staff of *The Motor* in 1962 and has spent his lifetime as a motoring journalist and author.

He was Grand Prix Correspondent of *The Guardian* and *The Observer* 1966-1980, motoring correspondent of *Town* (Haymarket) 1966-1968, and *The Observer* 1980-1982. While motoring correspondent of *The Sunday Times* 1982-1995, he won four Jet Media Excellence Awards including the outright title in 1988. Twice chairman of the Fleet Street Motoring Group, twice winner of the Montagu of Beaulieu Trophy presented by the Guild of Motoring Writers (GoMW) 1997 and 2008 for books on Saab and Bentley, he was also runner-up for his definitive work on world champion driver Jim Clark.

In a wide-ranging career, he was GoMW Regional Motoring Journalist of 2003. Eric compiled TV motoring programmes in the 1970s and 1980s for BBC and Thames TV, contributed regularly to *The Times, The Financial Times, The Daily Telegraph, The Scotsman,* classic car magazines, *Scotland on Sunday* 2002-2006 and *The Spectator Business* 2007. Broadcaster on BBC Radio 4, BFBS and World Service, in 2004 the Association of Scottish Motoring Writers (ASMW) honouring Scots who have achieved excellence in the field of motoring, presented him with the Jim Clark Memorial Award and in 2014 with its President's Award.

Author of: *Champion Year* with Jackie Stewart (Pelham, 1970), *The World of Racing Cars* (Hamlyn 1972), *The Guinness Guide to Grand Prix Motor Racing* (Guinness Superlatives, 1980), *Postwar Sports Cars* (Ebury, 1981), *Austin-Healey Sprite, MG Midget, a Collector's Guide* (Motor Racing Publications 1981, Heel Verlag 1991), *BMW, A Celebration*, (Pavilion UK and Orion USA, Heyne Verlag 1990), *Jim Clark, Tribute to a Champion* (Dove Publishing 1997 and Dove Digital 2011) and *Ecurie Ecosse*, (PJ Publishing 2007). Also under Dove Publishing's imprint, *Rover The First Ninety Years, Saab Half a Century of Achievement*, which gained the Montagu Award for 1997, *Honda the UK Story* and *High Speed Diary*. Dove's series of Eric Dymock Motor Books included definitive histories of Audi, Renault, Vauxhall, MG, Jaguar, Ford in Britain and Land Rover. *The Complete Bentley*, published in November 2008, won a second Montagu and is now included among Dove Publishing's ebooks, which include two volumes of Sports Car Classics, compilations of the author's features and motoring columns on sporting cars driven over 50 years.

MG Classics 3 is the last in the series, a most comprehensive account of every model under one cover with detailed specifications, performance and prices. It details MG company history, lists racing and record-breaking, is fully illustrated and crammed with reference material. Perfect for MG owners, fans and motoring historians. Authentic, accurate and distinctive, it is lively and highly readable. As with MG Classics 1 and 2, this edition is available as an ebook or paperback.

Researched by Eric Dymock, MG, and Austin-Healey owner, who road-tested and drove every MG featured, the MG Classics series is a unique source of facts, figures and analysis. Below, the author's concours-quality MGF.

Visit www.dovepublishing.co.uk to read more about Dove books and Eric Dymock.

1998 MGF Super Sports at Starkey's Bridge, once a bottleneck on the classic Donington track.

Printed in Great Britain
by Amazon

22112218R00073